DATE DUE

DEC 1 4 1993 5 3 6	
MAR 1 1994	
APR 0 7 1994	

FREE TRADE IN
AMERICAN-CANADIAN RELATIONS

By
Edelgard E. Mahant
Associate Professor
Glendon College, York University
Canada

AN ANVIL ORIGINAL

Under the general editorship of
Louis L. Snyder

KRIEGER PUBLISHING COMPANY
Malabar, Florida

1993

Original Edition 1993

Printed and Published by
KRIEGER PUBLISHING COMPANY
KRIEGER DRIVE
MALABAR, FLORIDA 32950
Copyright © 1993 by Edelgard Mahant

Library of Congress Cataloging-in-Publication Data

Mahant, Edelgard E. (Edelgard Elsbeth)
    Free trade in American-Canadian relations / by Edelgard Mahant ;
  under the general editorship of Louis L. Snyder. — Original ed.
        p.   cm.
    "An Anvil original."
    Includes bibliographical references.
    ISBN 0-89464-522-6
    1. Tariff—Law and legislation—United States.   2. Free trade—
United States.   3. United States—Commercial treaties.
4. Tariff—Law and legislation—Canada. 5. Free trade—
Canada. 6. Canada—Commercial treaties.   I. Snyder, Louis L.
II. Title.
KF6668.C32   1988.M34   1992
341.7'543'026673071--dc20
                                                              91-44703
                                                                  CIP

10   9   8   7   6   5   4   3   2

CONTENTS

LIST OF ABBREVIATIONS

AFL-CIO	American Federation of Labor-Congress of Industrial Organizations
CAW	Canadian Autoworkers
FIRA	Foreign Investment Review Agency
FTA	Free Trade Agreement
GATT	General Agreement on Tariffs and Trade
GDP	Gross Domestic Product
GNP	Gross National Product
ITC	International Trade Commission
MFN	Most Favoured Nation status
NAFTA	North American Free Trade Area
NDP	New Democratic Party
OECD	Organisation for Economic Cooperation and Development
UAW	United Autoworkers

PREFACE

States Free Trade Agreement has been
illions of words in the Canadian press,
books. In the United States, this Agree-
ment, which may a major departure in U.S. trade policy,
has received much less attention. This book seeks to redress the
balance to a limited extent, not by adding another million
words, but by giving Americans a brief and straightforward
introduction to this Agreement, its background, implementation
and possible consequences and successors. I have tried to give a
balanced picture, which includes Canadian as well as American
views of the Agreement. My hope is that Americans will find
this introduction to the subject useful, and that Canadians will
glean from it some knowledge as to American attitudes and
policies on this widely discussed subject.

ACKNOWLEDGMENTS

This book was written during a sabbatical from Laurentian University. It supported me, and to it I owe the greatest thanks. The Dean of Social Sciences at Laurentian University and later the research office at Glendon College also provided me with small grants which enabled me to get the book ready for publication. The Department of Political Science at the University of Toronto provided office space, excellent secretarial services, and most important of all, plenty of intellectual stimulation. Glendon College at York University enabled me to put the finishing touches on the manuscript.

Of people, three were particularly helpful. Greg Inwood, a Ph.D. student at the University of Toronto, did a lot of the legwork for the final stages of this manuscript and also provided much helpful criticism. Graeme Mount and David Leadbeater, both of Laurentian University, read chapters and provided many useful comments.

Dr. Louis Snyder and Ida Mae Snyder gave the manuscript an amazingly swift and thorough editing. The helpful staff at Krieger Publishing were just as fast and just as good. Any remaining mistakes are, of course, my responsibility.

DEDICATION

to my long-suffering and not always patient family,
Parkash, Sheila, Paul and Kam

INTRODUCTION

Free trade is a term laden with connotations and values. To some it means the freedom to produce, trade and prosper; to others, it means merciless competition and the continued oppression of the poor of this world. In North America, with our penchant for free enterprise and our liking for the word "free," we tend towards the first point of view.

This book places the 1988 Canada-United States Free Trade Agreement in its historical context. It describes and analyzes the political events and circumstances which led to that Agreement's conclusion. The last part of the book attempts an early evaluation of the Agreement's implementation, effects and consequences. The author's value system is that of a liberal humanist, who believes that when it comes to the evaluation of political and economic systems, the well-being of the individual human person is the measure of all things.

Free trade is meant to produce the greatest possible amount of goods for human consumption at the least possible cost. An American or Canadian might well answer that we have too much of goods and that it is time to move on to the fulfillment of other values. That may appear to be so north of the Rio Grande, but is not true in most of the rest of the world where millions and millions of people still lack the basic necessities of life. Even in the United States and Canada, there are people who lack food and many thousands who lack shelter.

The human race has not yet reached the time in its evolution where it can think of producing less. We need to produce more, at less cost to the environment, and we need to distribute what we produce much more equitably than we have in the past, not only among our own peoples, but among peoples the world over.

Can free and unhampered trade among nations play a role in achieving this aim? Classical economic theory says that free trade can help to produce more at the lowest possible cost. It is, however, silent on the question of distribution. It is at this point that politics enters the picture. In the twentieth century, we have expected political systems to distribute the necessities of life so as to ensure that everyone has the minimum needed for physical survival. Common sense would appear to suggest that if more is available the task of redistribution becomes less politically painful.

During the last twenty years, many people have begun to question the conclusions of classical economic theory with respect to trade. Two examples of the type of questions raised well illustrate this point. One of the assumptions of the advantages of free trade is that of long production runs. The idea is that the more a factory produces of a kind of good, the less each unit will cost. Recently, however, some experts in microeconomics have found that the largest firms can be unwieldy and inefficient. They speak of an optimum, rather than a maximum, size of firm. Computerized production techniques and concepts such as that of "just in time inventories" have also made it possible for a factory which produces fewer goods to produce at a lower unit cost than does a larger plant. A closely related concept is that of a "market niche," where a small or medium-sized firm can produce a specialized product at a lower cost or to a better quality than can a large company. A related issue is that of trade in services. Does it make any sense to speak of free trade in services? How much, if any, advantage is a larger market in the case of a service, such as transportation, hair-dressing or restaurants?

Another challenge to the idea of free trade comes from those who believe that free trade will only benefit the wealthiest and most powerful economies. They claim that under a free trading system, the wealthiest and most powerful economies have the advantages of buying power, high technology and a skilled labor force. These economies, also known as the "center," will suck resources out of the poorer economies, also known as the "periphery." Free traders reply that given a chance to produce freely and without hindrance the people of the peripheries can compete against those of the center. They point to the advantages of cheaper labor and lower overheads in many of the poorer economies.

Even if we accept the idea that free trade is a "good thing" (this is a question which is discussed further in chapter 1), another issue arises, that of regional versus world-wide free trade. The multilateralists say that only world wide free trade can reap the benefits of genuine free trade. They see regional trading blocs as the equivalent of powerful oligarchies which restrict the freedom to trade. Others say that free trade within regions is better than a reliance on national economies. They say that trading blocs at least expand the area of free trade, and in any case such trading blocs tend to expand and take in more nations.

Most important of all is the fact that we, as individual human beings, are not subject to the whim of blind economic forces. Though there are the occasional "acts of God," such as earthquakes, droughts or floods, overall, people create the economic forces which affect them and others. Economic events and trends do not happen because there is free trade, or any other governmental action or agreement. They happen because of the decisions of dozens of governments, thousands of individual businesses, and millions of individual consumers. The removal of a six per cent tariff may be much less significant than the reaction of managers, consumers and investors who hear that an agreement has been made and respond to that information. And people do not react only for economic reasons, that is only for material gain. People have other values, from national loyalty to religious convictions which may cause them, sometimes, not to make the decision that is economically most profitable. Other powerful factors include the force of tradition and lack of information. That is why the study of free trade is as much the subject of political science, history, psychology and marketing as it is of economics.

This book, in its study of the Canada-United States Free Trade Agreement, only touches on such basic questions about free trade, but they are questions that the reader may want to keep in mind. He or she may even attempt to formulate some answers.

Chapter 1 explores the historical idea of free trade and discusses some of the possible linkages between economic and political events.

Chapter 2 is a straightforward history of free trade between Canada and the United States.

Chapter 3 is a history of the specific 1988 Agreement, from the first suggestions for such a pact to its signing on January 2, 1988.

Chapter 4 is a summary of that Agreement.

Chapter 5 summarizes the national debate which preceded the Agreement's implementation, and for Canada, recounts the events which accompanied that debate.

Chapter 6 describes the implementation of the Agreement during its first two and a half years.

Chapter 7 makes an attempt to evaluate the effects of the Agreement; it also traces the beginnings of the talks with Mexico which may lead to the expansion of the FTA into the NAFTA. It is this expansion of the free trade area to include Mexico, a Third World country, (though not the poorest among them) which may allow future scholars to judge whether free trade can help to solve the major problem of our time, the disparity between the world's rich and its poor.

PART I

FREE TRADE IN
AMERICAN-CANADIAN RELATIONS

CHAPTER 1

THE IDEA OF FREE TRADE IN HISTORY

WHAT IS FREE TRADE? Most of us probably have some idea that free trade means the movement of goods across national frontiers without such restrictions as quotas, customs duties or export taxes. And until the 1950s, that is exactly what free trade meant. But during the last forty years, the composition of world trade has changed. Much trade now consists not of goods, but of services. Some of these services, such as the after-sales service agreements on a computer, are directly related to trade in goods, but others, such as advertising contracts, expert advice on environmental protection, or management expertise, are only indirectly related to the sale of goods.

What economists call the factors of production, capital and labor, have also become more mobile than they have ever been. Trillions of dollars of capital cross international boundaries every year. People do not have quite this freedom, but there has been a growing movement of people across international boundaries. While much of this is due to political events (such as the departure of foreigners from Kuwait in 1990), a significant proportion is due to economic factors. Despite government policies to the contrary, Latin Americans continue to come to the United States, and North Africans to France and Italy.

Under these conditions, free trade has come to mean more than just the free movement of goods across frontiers. "Free trade" now refers to various kinds of movements across national frontiers. It could mean free trade in goods and services, but it might also include capital and/or labor. When we encounter the term "free trade," we need to be careful to ascertain what the writer or speaker means by free trade.

THE ORIGINS OF THE IDEA OF FREE TRADE. Before the eighteenth century, those few individuals who had given the matter any thought assumed that it was governments which were responsible for the economy and trade. In ancient Egypt, Joseph became a valued adviser to the pharaoh by

3

advocating economic planning; he advised the pharaoh to save grain from years when production was high for the lean years which would follow when the weather was not so favorable. In the sixteenth century, King Henry V promised the people of France "a chicken in every pot."

By the 1700s, however, a number of people began to ask basic questions as to the role and purpose of government, and many of these questioners came to the conclusion that economies functioned best with a minimum of government direction and regulation. The best known of these economists was the Scot, Adam Smith (1723–1790), who described an economy as being guided by an "invisible hand," that is the impersonal forces of supply and demand. Smith's successor, David Ricardo (1772–1823), applied some of Smith's ideas to international trade. Using the mathematical logic of the theory of comparative advantage, Ricardo believed that he had demonstrated the economic benefits of free trade. (Reading 18 explains comparative advantage.)

Others were not so sure. Ricardo's ideas were at the center of the lengthy controversy about the so-called Corn Laws, which protected British grain farmers from foreign competition. Ricardians argued that the repeal of the duties on grain would allow other industries to pay lower wages. Lower wages would mean higher profits, and the resulting growth in investment would fuel economic growth. Advocates of the Corn Laws argued that the tariff kept in the country money which would otherwise go to foreign farmers. This money and the resultant prosperity of British agriculture would in turn ensure the prosperity of the British economy.

The Ricardians won this argument in 1846, when the British government repealed the Corn Laws. At that time, a similar controversy occurred in the United States. The high tariffs imposed in 1842 were reduced in 1846, only to be raised again in 1861. In the United States as in Canada the issue of free trade was and is linked to that of regional disparity. (*See Chapters 2 and 5*.) In the nineteenth century U.S., southerners, who for the most part sold semi-processed materials and bought manufactured goods, favored low tariffs, whereas easterners, who had to compete with British manufacturing industries, favored the protection of America's secondary industries.

The repeal of the British Corn Laws notwithstanding, the nineteenth century was not a time of free trade. By the end of the century every major industrial country, with the exception of Great Britain, was using tariffs to protect some of its major industries.

TWENTIETH CENTURY CONTROVERSIES ABOUT FREE AND FREER TRADE. While nineteenth-century economists and publicists stressed the economic benefits of freer trade, some among them also believed that the prosperity brought about by freer trade would lead to peace and understanding among nations. Twentieth-century thinkers have stressed this latter idea.

The American President Woodrow Wilson (1856–1924), for example, was a staunch advocate of lower tariffs. During his 1912 campaign for the presidency, Wilson argued that Americans had to buy from other countries if they wished to sell their own manufactured goods. After World War I broke out, Wilson began to speak of the political as well as the economic benefits of free trade. He argued that economic nationalism led to political hostility which in turn might lead to war. In his statement of war aims of January 8, 1918 (the Fourteen Points), Wilson included as Point 3, "The removal, so far as possible, of all economic barriers and the establishment of an equality of trade conditions among all the nations. . . ." Writing to Senator F.M. Simmons to further explain this point, Wilson stated:

The experiences of the past . . . have taught us that the attempt by one nation to punish another by exclusive and discriminatory trade agreements has been a prolific breeder of that kind of antagonism which oftentimes results in war. . . .[1]

Wilson's ideas found only a pale reflection in the peace settlement of 1919. Articles 23 of the League of Nations Covenant stated that the members "will . . . secure . . . equitable treatment for the commerce of all Members of the League." (The United States in any case did not ratify the Covenant.)

While the United States and Canada continued to raise tariffs during the 1920s and early 1930s (*see Chapter 2.*), prominent individuals in both nations voiced their belief in the benefits of freer trade. Cordell Hull, who served as President Franklin Delano Roosevelt's secretary of state from 1933 to 1944, was

[1] Arthur S. Link, ed., *The Papers of Woodrow Wilson*, Princeton: Princeton University Press, 1985, vol. 51, p.476.

one of the most articulate advocates of the political benefits of freer trade. On April 1, 1936, Hull recorded his impressions of a meeting with the British ambassador. This was at a time when the political tensions that were to culminate in World War II were becoming evident in Europe. Hull wrote that for several years governments had been pursuing the objective of a "purely nationalist economy" and that such a policy "inevitably means extreme, high political tension in many places at all times," that if the United States and other governments had been "functioning behind a suitable economic program during the past two or three years there is little doubt that Italy would not be on the rampage today." Hull repeatedly told the ambassador of his belief in "the beneficial effects on peace conditions of the liberalized commercial policy, such as we stand for." (*See Reading No. 1.*)

In Canada, Prime Minister Mackenzie King held similar views. The day after he returned to office in October 1935, King told Norman Armour, the American Minister (top ranking diplomat) in Ottawa that "unless something were done . . . to put an end to economic nationalism, . . . we were all in for real trouble. Economic nationalism not only meant isolation and ruination, but created bitterness and poisoned good relations between countries." King continued by expressing an interest in freer trade with the United States as well as the British Empire.[2]

Hull's and King's ideas were not put to the test. Although Canada and the United States entered into trade agreements with several countries (*see Chapter 2.*), Germany, Italy and other European countries continued on the path of what Hull termed "economic nationalism." Before World War II began, Hitler's government had used bilateral trade agreements (including some barter agreements) as well as currency manipulations to create an economic bloc in central Europe. Mussolini's Italy pursued a strategy of autarchy, that is trying to produce as much as possible in Italy and its possessions, regardless of the true cost.

After World War II, academics in large numbers turned their attention both to the possible benefits of freer trade and the

[2]Memorandum by Armour to Secretary of State, Oct. 24, 1935, in *Foreign Relations of the United States. 1935*, vol. II, *The British Commonwealth*, Washington: Government Printing Office, 1952, pp. 27–30.

supposed relationship between freer and more extensive trade and the political relations among nations.

Basing their ideas on sophisticated extrapolations of the classical theories, some economists believe that they can prove that even under conditions of imperfect competition, free trade will result in greater material benefits than would the protection of national industries. Others, however, point out that most of the theory of free trade is based on trade in goods; the same mathematical logic may not apply to trade in services.

Economists also make the case for free trade by drawing on historical evidence rather than mathematical logic. To support their case they cite the fact that since 1945 world trade has expanded more rapidly than has world income. (*See Reading No. 2.*) The annual economic report that President Reagan's advisors sent to Congress in February 1985 uses a number of historical examples to show that political entities which practice free trade become more prosperous than those who do not do so. (*See Reading No. 3.*) Historical evidence makes a strong, though not a conclusive case, for free trade.

FROM FREE TRADE TO FUNCTIONALISM. Political scientists have used some of the historical findings about free trade to build theories about the relationship between the growth of trade, transactions, and politics among nations. David Mitrany, whose first books were published in the 1930s, described a process of international cooperation which he called "functionalism." Mitrany believed that people are both rational and utilitarian; that is if they realize that a certain course of action will lead to a more comfortable life, they will choose that course of action. Mitrany's ideas relate primarily to technical problems such as cleaning up the pollution in a river which crosses international boundaries or finding a cure for a disease such as AIDS, a process which may be too expensive for any one country. But his ideas apply to trade as well. If economies of scale means that a car will cost less when one plant serves a market of three hundred million people than when it serves a market of one hundred million, then, according to utilitarian principles, most people will prefer the larger market because in that way more people could own cars, or those who own them could afford to replace them more frequently.

Mitrany believed that as people cooperate across international borders, authority for various human activities will gradually shift from national governments to various kinds of technical committees. In the case of the auto manufacturer mentioned above, safety and pollution control standards would no longer be set by any one national government or even a group of governments, but by committees of experts who would make decisions which would apply in all countries where the cars were sold. A similar process would apply to the testing of drugs or the banning of polluting chemicals, to mention only two possibilities. Eventually, formerly sovereign nations would be bound together by networks of cooperative committees, and national sovereignty will be so hollowed out that war will become technically impossible.

A later version of functionalism includes the concept of "spill-over." According to this idea, freer trade will force governments to harmonize their national legislation. If free trade is to reach a stage where customs officials no longer stop people and vehicles at national boundaries, taxation, gun control, and immigration rules in the participating countries will need to be similar. In this way, international cooperation will "spill over," from trade to other fields of governmental activity. This is the logic which underlies the European Community's 1992 program of complete economic unification.

The nation-state has proved to be more durable than the functionalists believed it to be. Technical regulation has impeded international trade as often as it has promoted it. National governments have agreed to abide by international standards for many activities, such as the protection of the ozone layer or the observance of fishing quotas; they have proved stubborn on others. The United States and Canada have still not agreed on controls for the emission of acid-rain producing chemicals, and within the European Community, it took more than thirty years before the German government, citing the supposed purity of German beer, reluctantly allowed beer from other member countries to be sold in Germany.

The functionalists may also be wrong in some of their assumptions about human nature. Sometimes people will prefer to endure hardship if they feel that is the only way to maintain their self-respect; witness the behavior of the citizens of countries which have been subject to economic sanctions. Or people may prefer to pay more for a car if that means that the citizens of their country, rather than those of another country, will be employed. In other words, predictions that people will prefer freer trade because of the material benefits it brings will not always come true. Sometimes people choose a course of action that does not bring them the greatest material benefit. It is because people can be motivated by a varying mixture of material and non-material advantages that prediction in the social sciences becomes so difficult.

After Mitrany, Karl Deutsch developed another type of integration theory. To Deutsch, trade constitutes but one of a number of "transaction flows" between countries. Other types of transactions include tourism, student exchanges, mail, telephone calls and computer hookups. Deutsch hypothesizes that an increasing quantity of transactions leads to a greater amount of contact between the peoples of the participating areas. Contact, in turn, promotes understanding or what Deutsch calls "mutual predictability." Deutsch led his graduate students in detailed empirical studies which demonstrated that increasing transaction flows and contacts preceded the creation of the United States and the (first) unification of Germany.

Deutsch's idea that transaction flows facilitate political integration is based on assumptions which differ from those of Hull and Mitrany, who believed that the material benefits of freer trade would lead to peace and international understanding. The difference is illustrated in the following diagram:

more trade, more contact, — — — — — — — — — — greater prosperity
more technical integration   and well-being

                    C   B

                        peace and
                  international understanding

Deutsch sees the benefits as flowing along line C; Hull and Mitrany saw them following lines A and B.

Deutsch also insists that mutual predictability and increasing contacts do not necessarily lead to political integration. He says that sovereign nations can co-exist in a "security-community," that is a group of states each one of which retains its sovereignty but whose citizens and elites have come to identify so closely with each other that war between them has become unthinkable. The Scandinavian countries, France and Germany, and Canada and the United States would appear to be contemporary examples of such security-communities.

Whether sovereignty can co-exist with increasing integration, as postulated by Deutsch, or whether increasing integration must lead to the hollowing out of sovereignty, as described by Mitrany, has formed an underlying theme of the debate about Canadian-American free trade. (*See Chapter 5.*)

Another criticism of integration theory may be relevant to the issue of Canadian-American free trade. Critics have pointed out that integration theorists assume that people will learn to get along better as they work together. This assumption seems to be based on the idea that there are no real conflicts of interests among states, but this may not be so. Consider the following example: If one country has energy resources and another has not, contact may make the people of the energy-rich country more willing to share with those of the energy-poor country. But it may not. The people of the energy-rich country, realizing their advantage, may become more determined to hold on to what they have.

FREE TRADE—AN ALTERNATIVE VIEW. Ever since David Ricardo first formulated his doctrine of free trade, free trade has had articulate and vocal opponents.

One major line of argument has come from nationalists who place the welfare of one group of people, their nation, above those of other groups. Some economic nationalists argue that the people of one nation, be it Estonia or Quebec, will be better off spiritually and materially if they take control of their own economy and develop it as best they can. While seldom put in such stark terms, this idea underlies the development plans of some Third World nations. Such plans have enjoyed some short term success, for example, in the case of China and Tanzania, but have not demonstrated their long term viability.

One major argument opposed to free trade comes from the "free trade is imperialism" line of thinking. According to this argument, free trade favors multinational corporations and countries with advanced technology. These critics of free trade point out that the gap between rich and poor countries has continued to widen; until 1979, the trade of rich countries also grew more rapidly than did that of poorer countries. Since 1980, the trade of the poorer nations has grown more rapidly than has that of wealthy countries, though the poorest nations did not participate in that growth. The World Bank claims that its studies show that free trade would benefit most of the developing economies, but that a small number of the poorest economies, such as those of Bangladesh and Tanzania, would suffer major losses.[3]

To explain why free trade may not always work as the classical economists had predicted, critics such as Gunnar Myrdal and Arghiri Emmanuel have argued that the classical doctrine was based on the assumption of the immobility of factors of production. Because in the contemporary world factors of production are in fact mobile, some countries suffer from a structural disadvantage, meaning that under free competition these countries would continue to lose jobs and employment, whereas other countries would continue to attract them. As a result some countries will become richer, while others will become poorer. (*See Reading No. 4.*) The only solution, these economists argue, is some kind of protection, such as minimum wage legislation or export taxes.

BILATERAL, REGIONAL OR MULTILATERAL FREE TRADE. The proponents of freer international trade have their own disagreements among each other. Is freer trade a good thing, even when it occurs among only two or a small number of countries, or must the number of countries be greater before the benefits can be realized? Cordell Hull, in the conversation with the British ambassador cited earlier, argued strongly for the idea

[3] World Bank, *World Development Report 1990*, New York: Oxford University Press, 1990, pp. 123 and 164.

of the most-favored-nation clause (MFN to the experts), whereby each country is obligated to charge every other country the lowest tariff it enacts against any one country. Hull was opposed to the preferential trading system among the parts of the British Empire and Commonwealth which existed at that time. Yet Hull promoted American-Canadian and Anglo-American trade agreements as steps in the direction of free trade.

A similar controversy persists today. Do blocs such as the European Community or the Canada-United States Free Trade Agreement, in fact, lead to greater productivity and to greater international harmony? Or do such regional blocs become exclusive areas which restrict international trade? Do such regional blocs not become embroiled in deeper and longer controversies than would individual countries? Critics such as David Leadbeater of Laurentian University in Canada have pointed out that the economic justification for some of the free trading blocs is suspect because these blocs tend to follow political and military alignments. During the Cold War years of 1947 to 1989, economic blocs tended to be either western (the European Community) or eastern (the Council for Mutual Economic Assistance).

After World War II, the United States led the world in the creation of a multilateral international trading system under the GATT (General Agreement on Tariffs and Trade), which until recently consisted mostly of western, developed economies. Since 1948, the creation of a number of regional economic blocs has meant that GATT negotiations have become more acrimonious and more difficult. The Dillon and Kennedy Rounds were easier than the Tokyo Round of the 1980s, and the current Uruguay Round has proved to be the most difficult of all. The European Community and the United States are facing off on the issue of agricultural subsidies, whereas the developed and developing countries are embroiled in a controversy about trade in services and intellectual property versus trade in goods. Other disputes continue between the United States and Japan.

The experience of GATT suggests that the existence of trading blocs makes the liberalization of trade more, not less, difficult. However, there are many who argue otherwise. The officials of the European Community maintain, and can produce statistics to show, that since its creation, the Community has become more prosperous and has bought more from other countries than it could otherwise have done. The *Economist* of September 22, 1990 (pp. S38–40) cites a study which claims that regional trading blocs which follow a liberal commercial policy will lead to greater gains in world trade than would a free multilateral trading system. The question of which is "better," multilateral or regional free trade, is one of the many social science questions that does not have a correct or perhaps even a knowable answer.

CONCLUSION. Careful analysis of the arguments for and against free or freer trade suggests that freer trade will lead to greater prosperity and the more efficient use of resources. Two provisos are necessary. The poorest countries in the world will need some kind of help and/or protection before they can participate in freer trade. Secondly, free trade needs to be supplemented by regional development policies within or, as in western Europe, among member states. Otherwise, industries will for the most part move into the already highly developed areas, creating problems of crowding and pollution and draining resources from poorer parts even of wealthy states. Governments may also choose to use social policy to relieve some of the pain, such as unemployment, caused by the transition to freer trade.

As to whether the prosperity brought about by freer trade will lead to international peace, the evidence is much less convincing. Repeated studies by many scholars have not found any correlation between the wealth of a nation-state and the peacefulness of its foreign policy. The evidence for the peace-promoting effects of increasing international transactions is somewhat more compelling. Studies by Deutsch and his disciples have shown that increasing contact among nations is often followed by deepening relations, which in turn leads to more contact. So to the extent that freer trade leads to contact among peoples, it may have some peace-promoting effects.

CHAPTER 2

THE HISTORY OF UNITED STATES-
CANADA FREE TRADE

BEGINNINGS. Until the American Revolution, all of British North America was a part of one colonial empire. From the time that they declared their independence from Britain, American leaders had to face the issue of their economic relationship with the rest of British North America. Their first response was an attempt to include Canada in the United States. American forces occupied the colony of Quebec late in 1775. In April 1776, Benjamin Franklin led a delegation of five to the American occupied city of Montreal. Their aim was to persuade English-speaking Canadians to join the American colonies in the revolt against Britain. Franklin's group received a cool reception and left two months later.

The Americans did not give up. When they drafted their first constitution (the Articles of Confederation of March 1781), they included the following statement: "Canada . . . shall be admitted into . . . this union; but no other colony shall be admitted into the same. . . ." (Article XI). Most Canadians, however, were not interested, and even if they had been, the British navy and armed forces stood by to prevent the realization of any such ideas.

Yet the idea of the annexation of Canada to the United States has persisted, and in the minds of both Canadians and Americans it has often been associated with the idea of Canadian-American free trade. On the American side, for example, some southerners opposed free trade in the 1850s because they thought it might lead to annexation. On the Canadian side, there were and are many who see annexation as a threat which lurks behind any talk of free trade. This was as true in 1911 as it was in 1988. (For discussion of the 1911 Free Trade Agreement, see page 21, below.) Other Canadians see annexation not as a threat, but as a goal, or perhaps an inevitability. Twentieth century opinion polls show that a sizeable minority of Canadians want

15

their country to become a part of the United States. In December 1989, for example, a *Maclean's* (January 1, 1990) poll found that 16 per cent of Canadians would like their province to become an American state; in Quebec and in Newfoundland one-quarter of the respondents gave that reply.

The fact that such a large proportion of the population is willing to join another country is surely unique in the modern world; it illustrates the love-hate relationship which has characterized Canadian attitudes to the United States since 1783. On the one hand, much of Canada's original English-speaking population consisted of those who left the new United States so that they could continue to be British subjects. Canadian suspicions of the United States, the idea that Americans are not only freedom-loving but also morally inferior, aggressive, violent and licentious has persisted in the Canadian psyche. On the other hand, Canadians admire America's achievements and her generosity, long to trade with her, and have, for the most part, followed an American lead in foreign policy. One could almost compare the Canadian attitude to that of a child to a strong parent. The young person is afraid of losing his or her identity, claims to despise some of the adult's values, yet admires others and in the end follows in the parental footsteps.

There is no similar identifiable American attitude to Canada and Canadians. Americans have sometimes found Canadians difficult and unnecessarily sensitive, but on the whole have just wondered what all the fuss is about. If Americans want to talk about trade, why do some Canadians insist on seeing a design on their existence as a country?

U.S. TARIFF POLICY. In his *Report on Manufacturers* (1789) the American Federalist Alexander Hamilton propounded an economic program designed to build up an American manufacturing industry by the exclusion of foreign (read British) manufactured goods. In fact, however, Congress and the presidents did not use tariffs as part of such a comprehensive program. During the nineteenth century, Whigs, who represented the industrial Northeast, favored high tariffs, whereas Democrats, who represented farmers, wanted lower tariffs. Primarily, however, tariffs were a major source of government revenue and were imposed not so much to protect American industry as to raise revenue for specific purposes, such as to pay for wars. In 1861, at the beginning of the Civil War, Congress raised some tariffs to 48 per cent. During the twentieth century, the tariff question remained a part of partisan politics, with Democratic administrations such as those of Woodrow Wilson and Franklin Delano Roosevelt favoring lower tariffs, whereas Republican administrations such as those of Warren Harding and Herbert Hoover raised tariffs. It was not until the 1980s that U.S. tariffs ceased to be a partisan issue. There are now free traders and protectionists in both major parties, with Democrats, on the average, probably more protectionist than the Republicans.

At all times, some major industries or other groups have lobbied for protection and have frequently succeeded in getting that protection. Historically, American tariffs have been high. They averaged 40 per cent during the nineteenth century and reached 60 per cent by 1930. Only since the 1948 creation of GATT have U.S. tariffs been lower than the Canadian tariffs. Most recently, attention in Washington has focused not so much on the protection of specific industries as on protection against specific countries. In 1989, for example, the U.S. government named Japan, India, and Brazil as sources of unfair trade.

American governments have also used tariffs for political, that is foreign policy, purposes. In 1793, Secretary of State Thomas Jefferson adjusted tariffs so as to favor France over Britain. In 1876, Congress agreed to a reciprocity treaty with Hawaii because Hawaii was believed to be important to American security, and in 1889, Secretary of State James Blaine attempted to negotiate a Pan-American customs union. During the Cold War, both Congress and the administration used tariff policy to reward or punish the Soviet Union and its allies; the Vanek amendment, for example, withdrew MFN status from the Soviet Union until it allowed the free emigration of Soviet Jews.

In short, American tariff policy has not usually consisted of a general program, but of a series of ad hoc measures, taken in response to specific events or perceptions of events. (Even the Truman administration's advocacy of a liberal international trading regime fits into this pattern since Congress refused to support Truman's policy and forced him to substitute the GATT for the International Trade Organization which his government had advocated.)

CANADIAN TARIFF POLICY. Unlike in the United States, where trade and tariff policies were made largely in response to the pressures of the moment, in Canada trade policies have formed a major part of governmental programs. The issue of free trade with the United States especially has been passionately debated and linked to fundamental issues such as the existence of Canada and the nature of its political culture.

During the 1830s and 1840s, Britain gradually gave Canada[1] the right to levy its own tariffs, and as in the United States, tariffs were a major source of government revenue during the nineteenth century. Nevertheless, Canadian governments espoused the idea of free trade with the United States until 1879, when, largely in response to the failure to obtain reciprocal free trade with the United States, Prime Minister Macdonald introduced the National Policy, a program designed to encourage the development of Canadian industry by means of tariff protection. (*See Reading No. 5.*) Efforts to negotiate free trade with the United States continued nevertheless; indeed, inducing the Americans to negotiate freer trade constituted one of the justifications for the National Policy.

From 1897 until 1973 Canada also had a preferential tariff for British Empire and/or Commonwealth countries. From 1911 to 1984, all Canadian governments, Liberal and Conservative, advocated and practised a considerable degree of protection of Canadian industry. Any exceptions were either partial (the treaty of 1935) or half-hearted.

FREE TRADE BEFORE 1911. It was not a coincidence that Britain allowed its North American colonies to set their own tariffs during the 1840s, when Britain itself adopted free trade. If Britain was to be a free trader, then colonial tariffs mattered little to Britain.

---

[1]Until 1867, Canada consisted only of what now constitutes southern Ontario and Quebec. From 1867 to 1873, five other provinces joined the Canadian federation. The remaining provinces joined in 1905 and 1949. In this book, Canada will refer only to the area called Canada. British North America is the correct pre-1867 term for what now constitutes Canada.

These new policies did matter to the Canadian colonies who, once they had lost their protected market in Britain, suffered an economic downturn as sales of timber and wheat to Britain dropped. Faced with a catastrophic number of business failures and high unemployment, a group of prominent young business-men and journalists met in Montreal in 1849 and signed the "Annexation Manifesto," asking that Canada be annexed to the United States. In this way, they hoped to obtain access to American capital and the American market. Within a year, a cyclical upturn in the economy began to revive Montreal's fortunes, and most of the signatories shamefacedly withdrew their support. It was the only time that such a prominent group of Canadians was to advocate annexation to the United States.

After Britain ended its preferential treatment of British North American goods, these goods still faced significant barriers at the U.S. border. Timber, a major Canadian export, faced a tariff of 20 per cent. As a result, free trade with the United States, or reciprocity as it was then called, had widespread support in the two Canadas (now Ontario and Quebec) and in New Brunswick, Prince Edward Island, and Nova Scotia. Lord Elgin, the Scot who was governor of Canada from 1847 to 1854, believed that only reciprocity could ensure Canada's prosperity, and that prosperity, in turn, would *prevent* the reappearance of annexa-tionist sentiment, a reversal of the idea that reciprocity might lead to annexation to the United States. Elgin convinced the British government to begin negotiations with the United States. (Although Canada could change its tariffs, it did not have full control of its foreign policy until the 1920s.)

In the United States, there was strong opposition to freer trade with Canada. Southerners who, except for the wheat growers of Virginia and Maryland, expected to gain from reciprocity, opposed it because they thought it might lead to annexation, which in turn would upset the balance between slave and non-slave states in the union. Wheat growers, timbermen and ship-builders feared Canadian competition. In 1853, both the House of Representatives and the Senate defeated a proposal for free trade in natural products when those who opposed free trade with Canada combined with those who wanted free trade in manufactured goods as well.

The administration of President Pierce favored reciprocity

because in return for freer trade the British North American colonies were willing to give liberal access to their fishing grounds. The administration hired a confidential agent, Israel Andrews, to wine and dine and bribe congressmen and Canadian politicians. But it was not until Lord Elgin arrived in Washington in May 1854 that negotiations succeeded. Elgin was known for his charming personality, and he used his charm, plus many bottles of champagne, to entertain members of Congress, especially those from the South. He convinced them, as he had earlier convinced the British, that the annexation of Canada would be *less* likely if reciprocity led to prosperity in Canada. After Elgin's ten days of partying, British and American representatives signed a treaty on June 5, which both houses of Congress adopted by August 4.

The Reciprocity Treaty of 1854 provided for free trade in most natural products and included 90 per cent of existing trade. It included not only Canada but also the four maritime colonies, and gave American fishermen almost totally free access to waters off British North America; British North American fishermen were to be allowed to fish as far south as the coast of Virginia. American citizens and British subjects were to have the right to freedom of navigation on the Great Lakes and St. Lawrence River systems.

Coincidentally or otherwise (historians disagree on this point), the early years of the treaty were years of prosperity on both sides of the border, but by 1859 this prosperity had peaked. To raise revenue and protect Canadian industry, the province of Canada imposed tariffs on American manufactured goods. The hostility this engendered among American manufacturers deepened considerably when, during the American Civil War, northerners saw Britain as sympathetic to the Confederate cause. In his study of Portland, Maine, the Canadian historian Graeme Mount has demonstrated how a mixture of patriotic motives together with mixed economic signals eventually led Maine's representatives in Washington to oppose the treaty (*See Reading No. 6.*) Similar processes were no doubt at work in the other states, and on March 17, 1865, the United States gave the government of Britain one year's notice of the abrogation of the treaty.

Eighteen hundred sixty-six was a good year for the Canadian

economy because American importers, anxious to buy their supplies before duties were re-imposed, greatly increased their purchases of Canadian goods. For the next fifty years, if not longer, Canadians associated free trade with the United States with prosperity. Government after government approached the United States in hopes of obtaining another treaty of reciprocity. Four of these attempts, in 1869, 1871, 1874–7 and 1896–7, reached the level of intergovernmental negotiations; the 1874–5 effort resulted in a draft treaty sent to but not considered by the U.S. Senate. Also, in 1887 and in 1890–91, Canadians attempted to begin negotiations on reciprocity but were rebuffed by the American government.

THE 1911 FREE TRADE AGREEMENT. During the twentieth century, the trade and tariff policy of both nations became more sophisticated. In 1897 Canada had introduced a lower tariff for Britain and her possessions (even though Britain still practised free trade and thus was not able to offer Canada any advantages). In 1907 the Canadian government added a third, intermediate tariff, which it could offer to countries who agreed to lower their maximum tariffs on Canadian exports. In a similar vein, the American Congress in 1909 adopted the two level Payne-Aldrich tariffs, higher for those countries which discriminated against American goods, and lower for those which agreed to give preference to American goods.

The 1907 Canadian and the 1909 American law forced both governments to charge each other the maximum rate of duty. The stage seemed set for a Canadian-American trade war, and that at a time of prosperity and growing trade. After the end of the Civil War, the percentage of American exports going to Canada had at times fallen below five per cent, but from 1901 to 1911, that percentage increased from 7.1 to 13.2 per cent. (*See Table 1.*) Canada at this time already took more than 60 per cent of its imports from the United States, although the major share of its exports still went to Britain. (*See Table 2.*)

A trade war would obviously be very costly to both economies. So it was the United States and not the Canadian government which in May 1910 suggested a free trade agreement between the two countries. President Taft and his more farseeing advisors were also concerned about the rise of imperial

Table 1

Major U.S. export markets, by ranking and percentage
of all U.S. exports, selected years, 1911–1946

Year	Market and Ranking		Comments
1911	1. U.K.	28%	
	2. Canada	13%	
1916	1. U.K.	34%	U.K. at war; U.S. not yet at war.
	2. Canada	11%	
1921	1. U.K.	21%	
	2. Canada	13%	
1931	1. U.K.	19%	
	2. Canada	16%	
1936	1. U.K.	18%	Imperial preferences went into effect at end of 1932, but appear to have made little difference.
	2. Canada	16%	
1941	1. U.K.	32%	U.K. at war; U.S. not until December
	2. Canada	19%	
1946	1. Canada	15%	Canada has been the U.S.'s most important customer since 1946
	2. U.K.	9%	

Source: United States, Department of Commerce, Bureau of the Census, *Historical Statistics of the United States: Colonial Times to 1970* Washington, 1976, part 2, pp. 903–905.

sentiment, that is the idea of greater unity among the possessions of the British Empire. Taft believed that free trade could keep Canada from becoming a part of this hypothetical imperial confederation.

The government of Prime Minister Wilfred Laurier was pleased with the American offer of reciprocal free trade. In spite of the general Canadian prosperity, the farmers of the West were clamoring for better access to American goods and the American market, and Laurier needed an issue for the upcoming general election. He was not about to give way to overeagerness.

Table 2
Canadian imports from the United States and
the United Kingdom, as a percentage of all Canadian imports,
selected years, 1883–1946

Year	US	UK	Comments
1883	45%	42%	Since 1883, U.S. has been chief supplier of Canadian imports.
1911	61%	24%	
1916	73%	15%	U.K. at war; U.S. not yet at war.
1931	63%	17%	
1936	58%	19%	Imperial preferences went into effect at the end of 1932, but appear not to have made much difference.
1941	69%	15%	U.K. at war; U.S. not until December.
1946	73%	10%	

Source: M. A. C. Urquhart and K. A. H. Buckley, eds., *Historical Statistics of Canada*. Ottawa: Statistics Canada, 1983, pp. G389–400 and G473–487.

Laurier told the Americans to wait until after the summer holidays.

Negotiations lasted only three months, from November 1910 to January 1911. The resulting agreement consisted of an exchange of correspondence followed by four schedules or lists. Schedule A listed a number of products on which both nations would remove all duties; included were most raw materials, but also some manufactured goods, such as cream separators, wire fencing, and thin rolled iron and steel sheets. Schedule B listed goods on which both sides would charge equal rates of duty. This list included a number of goods for which one side or the other wanted some protection, such as canned vegetables and motor vehicles in the case of Canada, barley for the United States. Schedule C was short; it listed semi-processed goods (aluminum and partly worked lumber) and raw materials (coal and iron ore) which the United States agreed to admit at preferential rates. Schedule D listed the goods which Canada agreed to admit at preferential rates: some processed foods, coal in large lumps, fruit trees, and cement.

It was a well balanced agreement. The fact that it met with much support and opposition on *both* sides of the border is ample evidence for that. In the United States, there were plenty of economic arguments for and against reciprocity, but there were also many political arguments for the agreement. The economic arguments *against* included damage to the lumbering and fishing industries as well as fears that American trusts would take over Canadian industry and thus become even more powerful. The economic arguments *for* included better access to Canadian raw materials, especially pulp and paper, a factor which weighed heavily with the many American newspapers which supported reciprocity. The political argument *for* consisted primarily of the opinion that Canada should be an American rather than a British nation. This was what President Taft meant when he made his famous speech in favor of the agreement:

Canada is at the parting of the ways. Shall she be an isolated country, as much separated from us as if she were across the ocean, or shall her people and our people profit by the proximity that our geography furnishes and stimulate the trade across the border. . . .[2]

In Canada, the reverse was true. The arguments *for* reciprocity were largely economic, but those *against* were political as well as economic. Canadian farmers and producers of semi-finished goods as well as consumers expected to gain from reciprocity. Canadian manufacturers and the major transcontinental railways opposed reciprocity and financed the campaign against it, but the most telling arguments used by Canadian opponents were the political ones. Canadian opponents of reciprocity claimed that if Canada accepted the agreement it would

[2]*Canadian Annual Review*, 1911, p. 72.

lose its Britishness and might even become a part of the United States. In this, the opponents were helped by a number of American commentators who speculated along similar lines. The speech which received the widest publicity in Canada was that by Representative Champ Clark, the Democratic majority leader in the House of Representatives. Clark said, "I hope to see the day when the American flag will float over every square foot of the British North American possessions, clear to the North Pole."[3] This was in February, before the Canadian debate had really begun. The *Canadian Annual Review* for 1911 collected twenty-six similar references from elected representatives throughout the United States. Such statements added emotional fuel to the debate among Canadians. There were Americans who intended to annex their country: the reciprocity agreement was only the first step.

The debate in the United States was short and successful. By the end of July 1911 both houses of Congress had passed and the President signed the bill. (The 1911 agreement set a precedent in that it consisted not of a treaty, which would have required Britain's signature, but of concurrent legislation to be adopted by both legislatures and signed by the two heads of state.)

In Canada the story had a different ending. Because of defections from his own party and an opposition filibuster, Laurier was unable to force the bill through the House of Commons. He called an election, and at the end an emotional campaign lost to the Conservatives, who opposed reciprocity. The Conservatives got 51 per cent of the popular vote, and obtained a large majority of the seats in the House of Commons. The new Prime Minister, Robert Borden, did not re-introduce the legislation; the American Congress did not repeal its legislation until 1919.

Why did Reciprocity 1911 fail? The money from the Canadian manufacturers and railway interests which financed the Conservative campaign helped, but the appeal to British imperial sentiment and thus the fear of American influence if not outright annexation were probably the most important factors. The electoral districts which supported Borden were also those

[3]*Canadian Annual Review*, 1911, p. 62.

which had the highest proportion of British-born immigrants. It was a time of much pro-imperial rhetoric throughout the British Empire.

The idea that free trade has political consequences formed an important part of the 1911 debate. American supporters and Canadian opponents agreed that reciprocity might lead to the annexation of Canada to the United States while President Taft and his advisors hoped that it would, at least, pry Canada loose from its close connection to the British Empire. Some Canadian Liberals also saw free trade as part of a more harmonious peaceful world order, and they cited a recent arbitration treaty between Britain and the United States as further evidence of this new order. Their case was weakened when the U.S. Senate voted down the Arbitration Treaty.

FROM WORLD WAR I TO WORLD WAR II. The idea that freer trade would have political consequences helped to defeat reciprocity in 1911, but for the next forty years it was political events which shaped the Canadian-American trade relationship. History offers just as many examples of political events changing economic forces as it does of the political consequences of economic trends, and the Canadian-American relationship is no exception.

The government of Prime Minister Borden continued the National Policy of protection of industry which it had promised during the 1911 election campaign. In 1914, Canada, but not the United States, entered World War I. Surprisingly, there were unemployment and excess capacity in Canadian industry during much of the war. After the United States became a belligerent in April 1917, the Canadian government (through the Canadian branch of the Imperial Munitions Board) made an agreement with the Ordnance Department of the United States in November of that year. By the terms of this agreement, the American Ordnance Department was to place all its Canadian orders with the Canadian representative of the Imperial Munitions Board in Washington. The representative would forward them to Canadian manufacturers and treat them just as if they were Canadian orders. This is an early example of the special relationship between the two countries; they did not treat each other as foreign governments.

The agreement did little to alleviate Canada's balance of payments or unemployment problems; that took political action in the form of a special appeal by Prime Minister Borden to President Wilson to have the United States place orders in Canada. The agreement was also undercut by Canadian manufacturers who sent their own representatives to Washington to lobby for orders.

The war had important indirect consequences for the relationship between Canada and the United States. Canada entered the war a British nation; by 1919 it had become an American nation, at least in its economic orientation. The cost of the war effort weakened the British economy. When Britain could no longer pay for its war orders from Canada, the Canadian government borrowed money on American capital markets. After the United States entered the war, the American government set aside $15 million dollars a month of the money it was lending Britain for purchases in Canada.

Because of the weakening British economy, Canadian-American trade grew in importance. (*See Tables 2 and 3*.) Also, by 1917 the United States had replaced Britain as the most important source of foreign investment in Canada, a status Canada, because the size of its economy, has not achieved in the United States.

The early 1920s were hard times in both the United States and Canada. The administration of President Harding responded with the Fordney-McCumber tariff of 1922. In 1927, Canada imposed duties on some manufactured goods. As the Depression took hold, the two governments became ever more protectionist. In June 1930 the U.S. Congress imposed the Smoot-Hawley tariff, which raised the *average* American tariff to 49 per cent and imposed some duties of over a 100 per cent. Canada retaliated in September 1930, in June 1931, and again later that year. The American government struck back in June 1932 by restricting imports of Canadian oil, coal, copper, and lumber.

Beginning with the Boer War of 1899 to 1902, Britain had gradually abandoned free trade. After World War I, the British government attempted to use trade policy to maintain the unity of its empire. In 1919, and again during the 1920s, Britain lowered duties on some imports from the empire. In conjunction with the special empire tariffs which Canada had introduced in

Table 3

Canadian exports to the United States and the United Kingdom,
as a percentage of all Canadian exports,
selected years, 1911–1946

Year	US	UK	Comments
1911	38%	48%	
1916	27%	61%	U.K. at war; U.S. not yet at war.
1921	46%	26%	
1931	41%	29%	
1936	36%	42%	Imperial preferences went into effect at the end of 1932 and seem to have made a difference.
1941	37%	41%	U.K at war; U.S. not until December.
1946	38%	26%	The U.S. has been Canada's most important export market since 1946.

Source: Edelgard Mahant and Graeme Mount, *An Introduction to Canadian-American Relations*. Toronto: Nelson Canada, 1989, pp. 317–318.

1897, this began the creation of a preferential British Empire trading system. At the height of the Depression, when it seemed that the American government was determined to cut itself off from international trade, the Canadian government took the initiative of inviting the British Empire and Commonwealth governments to Ottawa. They met during the summer of 1932 and created a preferential trading bloc among themselves, thus obligating Canada to discriminate against American imports.

In the meanwhile, Franklin D. Roosevelt became President in January 1933, and named Cordell Hull his Secretary of State. Both believed in free*r* trade, and Hull was only one of many

State Department officials who detested the idea of British Empire preferences which discriminated against the United States. In 1934, Roosevelt and Hull succeeded in persuading Congress to pass the Reciprocal Trade Agreements Act. This act gave the President the authority to negotiate tariff reductions of up to 50 per cent, but only with countries which were the United States' "principal supplier" of any one commodity.

Canadians saw their lack of access to the American market as a factor which intensified the Depression. In February 1933 both major parties in the Canadian House of Commons agreed to a resolution calling for a trade treaty with the United States.

Armed with support from their legislatures, the two governments began to negotiate in 1934. The process was time consuming since the Reciprocal Trade Agreements Act provided for lengthy consultations with American interest groups. By November 1935, Prime Minister King and President Roosevelt signed the first major Canada-American trade agreement to come into force since 1854.

By the terms of this agreement, Canada agreed to apply its lowest non-Empire duties to all American imports. In addition, Canada made concessions on other goods of interest to Americans, notably farm machinery, automobiles and parts, and ready-made clothing. Canada also agreed to cease the arbitrary valuation of goods for customs purposes. In return, the United States agreed to lower tariffs on goods of special interest to Canadians, including cattle, dairy products, lumber, fish, potatoes, and whisky. The treaty did not establish free trade, but it did remove most of the retaliatory tariffs imposed during the previous fifteen years.

Roosevelt and Hull were delighted that they finally had come to an agreement with one of the countries which had been a party to the 1932 Ottawa agreements, even though Canada maintained its imperial preferences. They next turned their attention to Britain. Ironically, as Tables 2 and 3 show, the imperial preferences seem to have done more to help Canada sell to Britain than they did to reduce U.S. sales to Canada.

Thus the Ottawa agreements had succeeded in diverting some trade. Canadians were now able to sell some goods, such as wheat, apples, and timber, to Britain more cheaply than were Americans. The British, whose flagging manufacturing industries were having difficulty competing in the United States, did not want to discuss the removal of imperial preferences. It was only when the political situation in Europe turned ugly (the rise of Nazism and the growing militancy of Germany, Italy's conquest of Ethiopia, and the Spanish Civil War), that the British government began to be interested in better trade relations with the United States. After lengthy preliminary talks in 1937, British-American negotiations began in April 1938.

Because of the imperial preference system, however, any British-American agreement of substance needed the consent and participation of Canada and to a lesser extent the other Dominions. Therefore, when negotiations began between Britain and the United States, they were paralleled by Canadian-American talks. The interplay of motives was fascinating. Hull and Roosevelt wanted trade agreements because they believed that economic cooperation could lead to prosperity and peace. The British were willing to contemplate an agreement which was not in their short-term interest (they had a huge trade deficit with the United States) because they were trying to buy U.S. political support with economic concessions. The Canadian prime minister, like Hull, believed in freer trade, but the Canadians were primarily interested in the economic benefits of freer trade for their own sake.

The upshot of all this was two further trade agreements by November 1938, one between Britain and the United States, the other between Canada and the United States. The Canadian-American agreement further liberalized trade between the two countries. Canada gained concessions on cattle, dairy products, fish, potatoes, and lumber. The Canadians made concessions on 236 goods, including fruits, iron and steel, and some paper products. This was not free, but freer trade.

The two agreements came into force by mid-1939, just two months before the outbreak of World War II disrupted all existing trade flows. There was not enough time to test Cordell Hull's idea that increased trade might prevent war.

World War II saw the closest economic integration that the United States and Canada had as yet experienced, but paradoxically also made trade between them less free than it had been before the war. The 1940 to 1945 economic collaboration of the two nations was government managed and government directed. Import controls, export controls, production [priorities, were just some of the many means the tw\ ments used to run the wartime economy. In the pr\ border became less significant. In many cases, such a\ the machine tool industry, Canada and the United States became one large market.

But that was not free trade. During 1940, for example, befo\ the United States entered the war, Canada experienced a severe shortage of American dollars. The government responded, among other actions, with the December 1940 War Exchange Conservation Act which forbade the import of many commodities and gave priority to sterling (British currency) countries for others. The passing of this act forced the Canadian government to ask the American government to waive some provisions of the 1935 trade treaty. The American government did so, and in return Canada left off the list of prohibited imports some items of special interest to Americans, such as fresh fruits and vegetables. This move away from free trade led to an interesting historical curiosity. American comic books were on the banned list of non-essentials. As a result Canadians produced their own comic books during World War II, a fact which has been a boon to collectors.

By the end of the war, a network of joint intergovernmental committees ran many aspects of the two economies, and by 1945 Canadian-American trade was greater than it had ever been. But this was government directed trade. (*See Table 4.*) Trade liberalization did not return to 1939 levels until 1946. By then, Roosevelt was dead, and Hull no longer was Secretary of State, but Mackenzie King, a *l*iberal and a *L*iberal, a trained economist and a believer in free trade, was still Prime Minister of Canada.

CANADA-U.S. FREE TRADE DURING THE POST-WAR YEARS. Wartime economic collaboration continued for about a year after the war's end, as the two nations dismantled the wartime economy in tandem, but then the Americans hoped to return to business as usual.

It was not that simple. As Canada struggled to rebuild its economy while also helping Britain, it ran out of American dollars in 1947, just as it had in 1940. The Canadian government once again restricted imports and foreign travel, but it also

Table 4

ajor sources of U.S. imports, by ranking and percentage
of all U.S. imports, selected years, 1901–1946

ιear	Source and Ranking		Comments
1901	1. U.K.	17%	Germany, France, Brazil,
	6. Canada	5%	and Cuba ranked ahead of Canada.
1911	1. U.K.	17%	Cuba was second.
	3. Canada	7%	
1916	1. U.K.	14%	U.K. at war; U.S. not yet
	3. Canada	10%	at war; Cuba was second.
1917	1. Canada	14%	From 1917–1985, Canada
	2. U.K.	10%	was largest single source of U.S. imports.
1931	1. Canada	13%	Japan was second.
	3. U.K.	7%	
1936	1. Canada	16%	Imperial preferences went
	2. U.K.	8%	into effect at the end of 1932, but seem not to have deflected Canadian sales to U.S.
1946	1. Canada	18%	Brazil, Cuba, Australia,
	6. U.K.	3%	and Mexico ranked ahead of the U.K.

Source: United States, Department of Commerce, Bureau of the Census, *Historical Statistics of the United States: Colonial Times to 1970* Washington: 1976. part 2, pp. 905–906.

asked the American government to revise the 1938 treaty by reducing tariffs on some Canadian exports. This led to Canadian suggestions of a comprehensive trade agreement, which the Americans countered with a proposal for a free-trade area. This appears to be the first ever mention of the idea of a free trade area. Paul Nitze of the State Department wrote of a special kind of customs union where the partners would retain their own tariffs vis-à-vis third countries.[4] (Since that time the terms *customs union* and *free trade area* have been defined in Article XXIV of GATT.)

After some initial hesitation, the Americans became quite keen to negotiate an agreement with the Canadians. At the beginning of the Cold War, closer relations with Canada seemed especially important; there was also still lingering resentment against imperial preferences, which some Americans saw as a barrier to the new multilateral trading system (the abortive International Trade Organization) they hoped to establish. Canadian-American negotiations began in January 1948, and by March the two sides had agreed on the content of the agreement (*See Reading No. 7.*) and were ready to start working on the exact treaty language. The agreement was to include the removal of all tariffs and most quotas, make special provision for agriculture and allow for the sharing of scarce resources in wartime. All the Canadians involved, including the Secretary of State for External Affairs, Lester Pearson, thought they had the basis of a good agreement.

Then Prime Minister King changed his mind. He credited divine intervention with his sudden new insight, but a more likely source was a full page editorial which, by coincidence, appeared in the March 15, 1948 issue of *Life* magazine. *Life* stated that "Canada needs 'complete and permanent economic union with the United States'."[5] The reaction in Canada was swift and largely negative. King ordered the negotiations stopped and threatened to reverse his planned retirement if they continued.

The 1948 negotiations are significant because they foreshadowed the contents of the 1987 agreement. Since then, Americans have been interested in freer trade not only for

---

[4]J.L. Granatstein, "Free Trade between Canada and the United States," in Denis Stairs and Gilbert Winham, eds., *The Politics of Canada's Economic Relationship with the United States* Toronto: University of Toronto Press, 1985, vol. 29, p. 40. (Published in cooperation with the Royal Commission on the Economic Union and Development Prospects for Canada.)

[5]Cited in Michael Hart, "Almost but not Quite: the 1947–48 Bilateral Canada-U.S. Negotiations," *American Review of Canadian Studies*, XIX (Spring 1989), p. 43.

access to the Canadian market but also for access to Canadian resources. In 1952, President Truman received the Paley Report, which specifically linked American military and economic security to access to resources and energy. In 1953, President Eisenhower's secretary of defense, Charles Wilson, had Eisenhower's enthusiastic support for Canada-United States free trade. The Canadian government would not hear of it; External Affairs Minister Pearson was terrified that the proposal might become public before the Canadian election of that year.

In addition to these discussions of overall free trade, the postwar years saw three examples of sectoral free trade, that is free trade in a specific industry. By the terms of a 1943 agreement, Canada and the United States had removed all trade restrictions on each other's agricultural machinery. This agreement remained in effect until it was subsumed by the 1987 free trade agreement (FTA).

A number of bilateral agreements, some dating as far back as 1917, have led to the gradual integration of the Canadian and American defense production industries. The various agreements have meant the standardization of military equipment have given Canadian firms the opportunity to bid on some American military contracts, and in the case of specific purchases by Canada of U.S. made equipment, have provided for "offsets," whereby some of the production work is done in Canada. In 1987, the two governments signed the North American Defence Industrial Base Organization (NADIBO) agreement. This agreement pulled together the many different agreements in defense production. It also signalled the formal exclusion of the defense industries from the Free Trade Agreement.

In 1965, the two governments made an agreement which provided for jointly controlled trade in automobiles and parts. Under this agreement, known popularly as the Autopact, Canada is guaranteed a share of the manufacturing process roughly in proportion to Canada's share of the market. The agreement applies to the three major American auto manufacturers (there being no indigenous Canadian manufacturers since the 1920s), but foreign car makers can participate if at least 50 per cent of the value added to their products is produced in Canada and the

United States. This agreement has been somewhat modified by the 1987 FTA, but is still in force.

CONCLUSION. The idea of Canadian-American free trade is almost as old as the separate existence of the two countries. Until 1911, it was usually Canadians who were interested in free*r* trade with the United States, and this interest was especially high in times of economic difficulty. Americans showed greater interest in free trade with Canada in times of prosperity and high national confidence, such as during the age of imperialism (1911). At other times, Americans such as Cordell Hull had political reasons for seeking free*r* trade with Canada.

American interest in free*r* trade with Canada grew with the Cold War, but as Canadian trade and investment dependence on the United States increased, Canadians and their government shied away from the idea of even closer economic links with the United States. This state of mind forms the immediate background to the Free Trade Agreement of 1987.

CHAPTER 3

THE ROAD TO
THE FREE TRADE AGREEMENT

CANADIAN ATTITUDES AND POLICIES, 1957–1983
During World War II and the first ten years of the Cold War, roughly until 1955, Canadian-American relations were as good and as close as they have ever been. The leaders of both governments perceived a common mission of defending the "Free World" against the "Communist threat." Concern about possible American dominance is not usually far below the surface in Canada, as is evident from the fate of the proposed free trade agreements of 1948 and 1953. This concern surfaced in 1957, with the election of the Diefenbaker government, which tried to offset Canada's dependence on the U.S. by once again deepening relations with Britain. This attempt failed.

In 1963, Canadian voters reaffirmed their adherence to the Western alliance when they elected the Pearson government which pledged to allow the stationing of American nuclear weapons in Canada, but concern about American economic influence continued to mount. Pearson's government tried but failed to introduce taxes which discriminated against American investment. (Too many Canadian interests would have been hurt in the process, an apt illustration of the intertwining of the two economies.) By the late 1960s and early 1970s, the Vietnam War and racial problems in the United States made Canadians ever more aware of how different they were from their neighbors. By the 1970s, a spate of books with titles such as Ian Lumsden's *Close the 49th Parallel: The Americanization of Canada* (University of Toronto Press, 1970) as well as public opinion polls showed an increasing public preoccupation with American economic influence.

When the Nixon administration announced a new international economic policy in August 1971 (*see below*), it did not grant Canadians the exemptions to which they had become accustomed. It was in response to this development as well as the rising nationalist tide in Canada, that Prime Minister Trudeau's Minister for External Affairs, Mitchell Sharp, proposed the so-called "Third Option" (1972), a policy of strengthening the Canadian economy and Canadian links with other countries so as to lessen dependence on the United States. In 1974, the Canadian government created the Foreign Investment Review Agency, which could monitor and in some cases halt or alter foreign investment proposals. In 1980 the fourth Trudeau government introduced the National Energy Program, intended to increase Canadian ownership and control of that sector. But by 1980, the force of Canadian economic nationalism had passed its peak. During 1981 and 1982 the government scaled back some of FIRA's authority; by the time of the 1982 recession, many Canadians were once again talking of freer trade with the United States.

Not that that option had ever been forgotten. Chapter 2 gave a brief history of Canada-U.S. free trade from 1854 to 1953. In 1967, two Canadian economists published a proposal for a Canada-United States free trade agreement. In 1975, the Economic Council of Canada, a government supported think-tank, suggested that the Canadian government consider the idea of a free trade agreement with the United States, and in June 1978, the Canadian Senate Committee on Foreign Affairs recommended that the Canadian government "seriously examine the benefits to be derived from free trade with the United States." (*See Reading No. 8.*) (Unlike its U.S. counterpart, the Canadian Senate has, in practice, not been a very influential part of the Canadian political system.)

AMERICAN ATTITUDES AND POLICIES, 1945–1984. While it is relatively easy to describe Canadian attitudes and policies toward the United States, it is not usually possible to identify an American policy toward Canada. Instead Canada needs to fit into the larger picture of American commercial and foreign policy.

As the predominant economic power in the world after World War II—in 1946 the goods and services produced in the United States made up nearly half of the entire world's production—the American people felt generous toward others and were optimistic enough to believe that they could benefit from a liberal, multilateral trading system. That is why in 1948 they led the world in the creation of the GATT, the General Agreement on Tariffs and Trade (although even the GATT is a scaled down version of the abortive International Trade Organization, which Congress would not approve).

As the war-ravaged economies of Japan and Europe rebuilt themselves and as some Third World nations began to take their place in the world economy, the relative importance of the United States as an economic power declined. The Vietnam War and high defence spending further weakened the American economy. In 1971 the United States experienced its first merchandise trade deficit in over a century, by 1982 its balance of payments was in deficit, and in September 1985 the U.S. officially became a debtor nation (meaning that all the assets foreigners held in the United States were greater in value than the assets Americans own outside the U.S.).

American governments responded by trying to reduce American responsibilities within the international economic system. In August 1971 the Nixon administration ended the system by which the U.S. dollar had been the "reserve currency" against which all others were measured. Many members of the American policy-making elite were beginning to have second thoughts about the multilateral trade and payments system, which they believed others had taken advantage of to the disadvantage of the United States. Economists and members of the policy-making elite came forward with various proposals for managing foreign trade and protecting and promoting American industry, a policy sometimes known as getting "the fustest with the mostest." Among the departures from multilateral free trade, regional trade blocs were one of the most widely canvassed options. The Europeans had their European Community, the Latin Americans were organizing various free trade areas, and governments in Africa, Asia and the Pacific were discussing similar arrangements. Why should the United States not do likewise?

Proponents of regional trade blocs usually agree that multilateral free trade is the most economically advantageous course of action for all participants, but they argue that since other governments are not following the principles of multilateral free trade, the American government needs to take steps to protect

American interests. They say that free trade areas can become building blocks and/or bargaining chips during multilateral negotiations, can set a precedent of free*r* trade, and can provide the United States with expanded markets while multilateral negotiations drag on. In the 1930s, it had been accepted almost without question that bilateral free trade agreements were useful stepping stones to further free trade, but since the 1970s there have been sharp disagreements between two groups of American economists: those who contrast bilateralism, which they see as potentially trade restricting, with multilateralism under GATT, which they see as the arena for genuine free trade, and those who favor bilateralism as an alternative to multilateral freer trade.[1] (*Reading No. 9* reproduces the principal arguments of the bilateralists.)

Bilateralist thinking entered into U.S. government policy with the Reagan administration. In 1981, David McDonald, the Deputy U.S. Trade Representative, said, "We may have pressed multilateralism to the limits . . . our reactions will be somewhat . . . more reciprocal than they have previously been," and in February 1985, the United States President's Council of Economic Advisers recommended that if multilateral negotiations stalled, the U.S. government should turn to bilateral trade negotiations.[2]

Lately the word *plurilateralism* has appeared in this debate. Plurilateralism refers to the creation of economic blocs such as the European Community or the Canada-United States-Mexico free trade area. Thus plurilateralists, like bilateralists, believe that the United States should experiment with alternatives to the GATT type of multilateralism.

A bilateral trade agreement with Canada provided the best possible testing ground for the ideas of the bilateralists. Canada was the United States' largest trading partner, so that free trade

---

[1] For an excellent summary of this debate, see the chapters by Anne Krueger and Rudiger Dornbusch in Robert Lawrence and Charles Schultze, eds., *An American Trade Strategy for the 1990s*. Washington: The Brookings Institution, 1990.
[2] Cited in John H. Jackson, "Multilateral and Bilateral Negotiating Approaches for the Conduct of U.S. Trade Policies," in Robert M. Stern, ed., *U.S. Trade Policies in a Changing World Economy*, Cambridge: The MIT Press, 1988, 383; *Economic Report of the President*. Transmitted to the Congress February, 1985, Washington: United States Government Printing Office, 1985, 125.

with it would affect a large proportion of U.S. trade. Even the multilateralists agreed that free trade with Canada might be an exception that should be allowed. According to Anne Krueger, "geographic and other links between Canada and the United States would permit the formation of a free trade area without abrogation of the spirit of the open, multilateral trading system."[3] In 1982, Sperry Lee of the non-government Canadian-American Committee even produced a draft of a Canada-United States free trade agreement.

These ideas did not take long to find their way into Congress. Section 612 of the 1974 Trade Act stated that it is "the sense of Congress" that the United States should enter into a trade agreement with Canada so as to guarantee the "continued stability" of the two economies. The clause continued by authorizing the President to "initiate negotiations with Canada to establish a free trade area," the results of such negotiations to be submitted to Congress. No presidential action appears to have resulted.

There was also some discussion in Congress of a "North American Energy Alliance," but no resolutions on that subject were adopted. (See, for example, Senator Durkin's statement of April 5, 1979.) When Congress adopted the 1979 Trade Act, it retained the section on free trade with Canada, but amended it by requiring the President to study such a free trade area over the next two years. The amendment referred not to Canada but to the "northern portion of the western hemisphere." (This strange wording may have been meant to include the Danish and French possessions off Canada's coasts.) The amendment specifically mentioned agriculture and energy as sectors to be studied. The administration completed such a study in July 1981, but concluded that a free trade area with Canada was not practical at that time.

Congressmen and Senators were not the only ones to be thinking about free trade with Canada. In November 1979, when Ronald Reagan announced his candidacy for the presidency, he included in his speech a call for closer relations with Canada and Mexico. These "three countries," he said, "possess the assets to make it [the continent] the strongest, most

[3]Krueger in Lawrence and Schultze, 1990, 91.

prosperous and self-sufficient area on earth." (*The New York Times*, November 14, 1979)

In 1982 the Reagan administration attempted to get GATT to start negotiations on topics of special interest to Americans, such as freer trade in services and agriculture and protection of foreign investment and intellectual property. A large delegation, including several senators and congressmen, formed part of the negotiating team, but the attempt failed in November 1982 and left several of the participants convinced that multilateralism was not working.

Also, in 1982 the Reagan administration announced the Caribbean Basin Initiative, a series of aid and trade measures which constituted a departure from multilateral free trade. Enacted in 1983 and 1984, the trade measures of the Initiative gave Caribbean countries a limited degree of preferred access to the American market. The Initiative, though, was primarily political in nature. It was meant to strengthen the economies of the Caribbean nations so as to make them less vulnerable to supposed Cuban subversion.

In 1984 Congress returned to the idea of bilateral free trade. The 1984 Trade Act authorized the President to negotiate free trade areas with Israel and Canada, provided that he first obtain so-called "fast track" authority from the Congress and later submit the entire agreement to Congress for approval or rejection. In an explanatory report to the Senate, dated June 12, 1984, Senator Robert Dole, on behalf of the Senate Finance Committee, explained that the initiative for these free trade areas had come from Israel and Canada, but that "the committee believes that the economic interests of the United States clearly favor pursuing the proposed negotiations at this time." Congress adopted the amended act, and the United States concluded a free trade agreement with Israel in 1985. Like the Caribbean agreement, that with Isreal is primarily political in nature; it is meant to show support for a faithful ally. The agreement with Canada has a longer and more complex history.

CHANGING ATTITUDES AND A CHANGE IN POLICY IN CANADA, 1982–1985. Throughout their history, Canadians have tended to turn to the United States in times of economic difficulty. The Third Option had been applied only haphazardly, as the Canadian government became preoccupied with other issues, such as constitution-making. (For discussion of the Third Option, see page 38, above.) Canada's dependence on U.S. trade remained what it was. By the time of the recession of 1982, Canadian economic nationalism appeared once again to be a luxury the country could not afford. That year a report by the Canadian Senate again suggested that the government investigate the idea of free trade with the United States.

More importantly, the idea of free trade with the United States now had the support of significant sectors of the Canadian business community. During 1983 and 1984, the Canadian Chamber of Commerce, the Business Council on National Issues, and the Canadian Manufacturers Association all called on the government to consider free trade with the United States. This represented a significant change of policy, particularly on the part of the manufacturers who since John A. Macdonald's days had sheltered behind Canada's tariff walls. Two main factors accounted for this change in policy. By the 1980s, almost three-quarters of Canada's foreign trade was with the United States. There seemed little point of looking elsewhere to offset Canada's dependence on that one market. Instead the best way for Canadian firms to shelter themselves from U.S. protectionism appeared to be to get under the blanket with the Americans. The other factor consisted of the links between American and Canadian multinational companies. The subsidiaries which American firms had established in Canada, in many cases in order to get inside the Canadian tariff walls, now wanted to trade freely with other parts of the same company. So these same intercorporate links led to increasing pressure for United States-Canada free trade.

The Trudeau government, which had been following a nationalist policy of limited controls over investment and energy, responded cautiously. In August 1983, Gerald Regan, the Minister for International Trade, repeated the traditional Canadian belief that general free trade with the United States might lead to political dependence, but he added that sectoral free trade, such as that which already existed in the auto industry, might be attempted for several other industries. Americans were sceptical of the idea of sectoral free trade. They believed that free trade with Canada should include most industries; in the words of two

American economists, "We conclude that the prospects for Canada-U.S. trade liberalization are best if the design is bold."[4] But the American government did not want to refuse an initiative which might lead to freer trade with Canada. It, therefore, agreed to the Canadian suggestion, and in February 1984, the Canadian Minister for International Trade and the U.S. Trade Representative announced that negotiators would begin to work on four sectors: steel, computer services, urban mass transit equipment, and agricultural equipment. (This last had been the subject of a previous sectoral agreement.)

Before negotiations could make much progress, a Canadian and then an American election campaign intervened. The American election returned the same president, but the Canadian election of September 4, 1984, brought to power a new government led by the Conservative, Brian Mulroney. His election was the one factor which made a Canada-United States free-trade agreement possible and even probable.

Traditionally, the Canadian Conservative Party had been both opposed to freer trade and to closer relations with the United States. As late as 1983, Brian Mulroney, the party's newly elected leader, spoke against Canada-United States free trade, which he called a threat to Canada's sovereignty. Yet, Mulroney favored closer relations with the United States. In June 1984, while still leader of the opposition, he visited Washington, where he was seen by President Reagan as well as other top U.S. officials. While in Washington, Mulroney attacked the Canadian government for allowing relations with the United States to deteriorate. During the Canadian election campaign which followed in July and August, Mulroney and other senior Conservatives called for more foreign investment, but did not mention free trade with the United States.

PREPARING PUBLIC OPINION. The first mention of free trade from a Canadian government source came in January 1985 (strictly speaking the Senate is a part of Parliament, not of

---

[4]Gary Clyde Hufbauer and Andres James Samet, "United States Response to Canadian Initiatives for Sectoral Trade Liberalization, 1983–1984," in Dennis Stairs et al, *The Politics of Canada's Economic Relationship with the United States. Macdonald Commission Study.* Toronto: University of Toronto Press, 1985, vol. 29, 202.

the government) when the new Conservative government issued a "discussion paper" which concluded in almost hesitant language that free trade with the United States might be good for the Canadian economy. By this time, the idea was the subject of a widening public debate in Canada, and thus became a natural subject of Mulroney's search for better relations with the United States.

In the United States, the passing of the Omnibus Trade bill of October 1984 was followed by hearings by the International Trade Commission. In March 1985, the ITC reported that only two of the thirty-five industrial groups consulted expected to be hurt by a free trade agreement with Canada. The National Manufacturers Association studied free trade with Canada during the first half of 1985 and reported favorably on it. A number of officials from the Office of the United States Trade Representative also spoke in favor of the policy at that time.

The two governments must also have been talking about free trade in their preparations for the March 1985 Mulroney-Reagan summit meeting, but little of these discussions has become public. When the two leaders met in Quebec City on March 17–18, 1985, the several communiqués they issued included one on "trade in goods and services." The communiqué called for:

- the reduction and elimination of "existing barriers to trade"; the facilitation of investment;
- "national treatment . . . with respect to government procurement";
- a "market approach to Canada-United States energy trade";
- "facilitation of travel for business and commercial purposes";
- "co-operation to protect intellectual property rights."

The Canadian Minister for International Trade and the U.S. Trade Representative were to report within six months as to how these aims could be achieved.

The Canadian government moved slowly and carefully. The Prime Minister had not yet mentioned free trade in public. As late as July 7, 1985 he spoke of "enhanced" trade with the United States. The official change in Canadian policy came in September. On September 5, 1985, the Royal Commission on the Economic Union and Development Prospects for Canada, which the previous Liberal government had appointed, issued its multi-volume report. Included was a recommendation, backed by two volumes of studies, for free trade with the United States. (*See Reading No. 10.*) With such authoritative backing, the Prime Minister felt that he could at last commit his government. On September 26, 1985 he announced in the House of Commons that he had telephoned President Reagan to request that negotiations for a Canada-United States free trade agreement begin. The Prime Minister did not use the term "free trade." Instead, he spoke about "the broadest possible package of mutually beneficial reductions in tariff and non-tariff barriers." (*See Reading No. 11.*) At the same time, he submitted to the Commons the report the communiqué of March had requested. It also, of course, favored free trade negotiations.

Three factors above all others motivated this historic change in Canadian trade policy. First and foremost the Canadian policy represented a response to the perceived rise of protectionism in the United States. If the United States were to turn away from multilateral trade liberalization, Canada, which is so dependent on the U.S. market, would suffer first and most. In a speech to the Halifax Board of Trade on March 19, 1985, the Canadian Minister of International Trade, James Kelleher, claimed that during the last few years, more than one thousand protectionist bills had been introduced in the American Congress, and in his statement to the Commons Mulroney stressed the need for access to the U.S. market. Second, many Canadian Conservatives as well as some economists believed that a trade agreement with the United States would be good for the Canadian economy. Freer trade would force Canadian industries to become more competitive, while American investment capital would help to restructure Canadian industry. In this sense, the movement toward bilateral free trade formed a part of the neo-conservative stress on competitive, capitalist economies. Third, the Canadian government believed Canada to be isolated in a world of trade blocs. The fact that Canada was the only industrialized country without assured access to a market of more than thirty million people was often mentioned.

The change in policy was less dramatic in the case of the United States, which had already negotiated the trade agreement with Israel and the Caribbean Basin Initiative. Yet, an agreement with its major trading partner constituted a turning away from multilateralism, in which many in the United States administration had lost faith. An agreement with Canada would demonstrate that the United States had alternatives and would also offer concrete economic advantages. In September 1985, the administration statement on international trade policy suggested that a "bilateral free trade agreement" could "complement our multilateral efforts." During the same month, a report by Clayton Yeutter, the United States Trade Representative, recommended very hesitantly that the United States begin negotiations with Canada. (*See Reading No. 12.*) Such an agreement would also promote other foreign policy objectives. James Baker, then Secretary of the Treasury, stressed the security aspect of access to Canadian resources such as energy, whereas President Reagan saw free trade in terms of a reward for a good ally. His letter of April 1986 asking for Senate authorization to negotiate with Canada pointed out that Canada had been very supportive of U.S. concerns on international terrorism and East-West relations.[5]

The period from the time of Mulroney's announcement until the signing of the agreement on January 2, 1988 can be divided into two segments. The first, the pre-negotiation stage, lasted from September 1985 until April 1986, when President Reagan obtained the "fast track" negotiating authority from Congress. The actual negotiations began on May 21, 1986 and lasted until the beginning of December 1987.

THE PRE-NEGOTIATION STAGE. During this stage, the two governments put their negotiating teams in place. In November 1985, Prime Minister Mulroney named Simon Reisman as chief Canadian negotiator. Reisman was an experienced international trade negotiator, and as a former deputy minister of finance had also held one of the highest level civil service posts in Canada. Reisman assembled a team of over a hundred experienced experts. The Canadian government also put into place an elaborate system of communication between govern-

[5]The administration statement is cited in Richard Snape, "Is Non-discrimination really dead?" *World Economy*, vol. XI (March 1988), 11; James Baker, "The Geopolitical Implications of the U.S.-Canada Trade Pact," *The International Economy*, Jan.-Feb. 1988, 39; *The Washington Post*, April 22, 1986.

ment and industry. Committees of industrial representatives were set up to advise the negotiators as to how various industries might be affected by the proposed provisions of the agreement. Consultations with the provincial governments were also arranged. The federal government had also consulted major industrial groups before the announcement in the House of Commons, but believed further consultations during the negotiations to be necessary so as to maintain the widest possible base of support.

In February 1986, President Reagan appointed Peter Murphy to head the American team. Murphy had been the deputy head of the U.S. delegation to GATT, but had recently been on sick leave and was thus perhaps somewhat out of touch. He was also young and relatively junior within the Washington hierarchy of trade negotiators. Murphy assembled about forty experts as well as some part-time advisors on leave from various U.S. government agencies. The U.S. government already had a system by which industries were consulted about international trade negotiations, and Murphy made use of that system. It is obvious that the U.S. government attached less importance to the negotiations than did the Canadian government.

President Reagan needed to obtain negotiating authority from Congress. Under the so-called "fast track procedure," the President, having duly notified Congress of his intention, could negotiate an agreement which Congress would have to approve or reject in its entirety *unless* either the House Ways and Means Committee or the Senate Committee on Finance voted a resolution to tell the President he did *not* have the authority to negotiate. On December 10, 1985, the President wrote to Congress specifically asking for authority to negotiate a bilateral free trade agreement with Canada. The House Committee chose to devote its time to other issues, but the Senate Finance Committee began to deal with the President's request on April 11, 1986, just twelve days before the President would have had his authority by default.

It seemed at the beginning of the committee debate that a majority opposed the negotiations. The Canadian press counted votes daily and gave the committee the coverage normally reserved for the Stanley Cup or the World Series. The actual debates were much less exciting. The senators discussed potash, timber, potatoes, fish, uranium, and other specific products. The White House exerted considerable pressure on the senators. On April 23, the last possible day, they voted ten for negotiations and ten against, which by Senate rules means that the President had his authority.

THE NEGOTIATIONS. Neither government issued a formal statement of its negotiating objectives. Such matters are considered state secrets which could be of use to the other side. However, various statements by leaders of both sides make it possible to piece together a reasonable summary of the two governments' principal negotiating objectives.

Both governments had general objectives which pertained to the proposed agreement as a whole as well as more specific objectives with respect to the agreement's content. The American administration's general objectives related to its over-all trade and foreign policy. With respect to trade policy, the U.S. administration wanted to see an agreement which included subjects such as services, investment, and intellectual property as an example for the ongoing GATT talks. Furthermore, a successful FTA would give the United States its own regional trading bloc, or at least the beginning of its own regional trading bloc. Such a bloc would be a useful support during GATT negotiations and would also provide a fallback position if GATT negotiations failed.

As for specific goals, the American government sought unhindered access to the Canadian market for American goods, services, and especially investment capital. The Americans were particularly concerned about the removal of non-tariff barriers such as restrictions on government procurement and Canadian provincial liquor board regulations. They also wished to deal with intellectual property, such as patent rights for pharmaceuticals and copyrights for television programs, and they wanted to limit the Canadian government's use of what they called subsidies. These subsidies were not defined, but they probably included regional development grants, aids to specific industries such as timber and agriculture, some cultural programs, and perhaps also social programs. The Americans also sought unhindered access to Canadian resources, especially energy. Members of Congress had their own objectives with respect to the negotiations. They were concerned about unfair competition, in which they included measures such as unemployment insurance for fishermen. They wanted the Canadian dollar to have a higher value in relation to the American dollar, and they wanted changes to the Autopact.

The Canadian side had fewer general but more specific aims. What is more, the Canadian government's general objectives related to domestic rather than foreign policy. The Canadian government sought to make the Canadian economy more competitive by making it more like the American, that is oriented toward free enterprise and competitiveness. The government believed that American competition would force Canadian business and labor to become more productive and cost conscious. An agreement on investment controls and energy would prevent future Canadian governments from implementing nationalist measures, such as those introduced by the last Trudeau government. In this way, an agreement with the United States would allow the Conservative government to impose its agenda on future Canadian governments. A free trade agreement with the United States would also address the problem of interprovincial barriers to trade *within* Canada because an international agreement made by the federal government would require all provinces to take the necessary implementing measures.

As for aims relating specifically to the negotiations, the Canadians wanted, above all, to have unhindered access to the American market for goods and most services, but they wanted trade barriers to be dismantled gradually. They wanted access to the U.S. market for government procurement. The Canadians also wanted to preserve the 1965 Autopact, and to exclude cultural, regional, and social programs from the negotiations. Above all, they sought a binding dispute settlement procedure which would exempt Canadians from the whims of American foreign trade law and of the various government bodies which interpret it.

There were thus some common, but also some conflicting goals. The official negotiations began in Ottawa on May 21, 1986 and continued from then until October 5, 1987, the date by which President Reagan had to submit a text to Congress. What is known about the negotiations consists almost entirely of speculation mostly in the Canadian press.[6]

The negotiations were long and hard. The two sides were far apart on many issues, and the atmosphere was poisoned by a series of unrelated bilateral trade disputes, such as the U.S. imposition of a tariff surcharge on Canadian cedar shingles (June 1986), the U.S. threat to impose a tax on Canadian softwood (October 1986) which forced the Canadian government to tax itself (December 1986), and the Canadian imposition of duties on U.S. computer parts (June 1986) and corn (November 1986). The Democratic victory in the 1986 off-year election enabled the American side to threaten the Canadians with a recalcitrant Congress. A number of tactless comments by members of Congress caused further deterioration in the negotiating climate. In April 1987, for example, Senator Matsunaga said to a Canadian audience, "the sooner your culture and ours can blend, the better it is going to be for both our countries," and in June a congressional staffer wrote that Bill Merkin, the deputy American negotiator, had promised to reduce the Auto-pact to a mere shell.[7]

By May 1987, the talks appeared to have made little progress. The Canadians insisted on the dispute settlement mechanism, and the Americans on freedom to invest in Canada. Neither side would give way. When Reisman reported to provincial premiers in July, he had next to nothing to tell them.

Although there undoubtedly were genuine disagreements, it is also possible that last-minute pressure toward the October 5 deadline was a tactic the two governments used to get agreement from reluctant legislators and provincial governments. The Canadian press reported as early as April 1987 that there would be a draft agreement by October 4, but that the final text would be ready only in December.[8] In October, this draft agreement,

---

[6] "A Big Deal: The Canada-US Free Trade Agreement," in Robert M. Campbell and Leslie A. Pal, *The Real World of Canadian Politics*, Peterborough: Broadview Press, 1991, 187–266 does the best job putting together all these press accounts.

[7] *Canadian New Facts*, April 1–15, 1987, 3608, and June 16–30, 1987, 3649. The Autopact is the 1965 agreement which establishes a managed trade regime for the American and Canadian auto industries.

[8] *Canadian News Facts*, April 1–15, 1987, 3607.

cobbled together at ten minutes to midnight, was presented as a last minute compromise, put together, *faute de mieux*, because there was no time to draft the final agreement.

The two sides had produced a draft agreement on August 28, though, that included bracketed sections, that is sections on which there was no agreement. Nevertheless, Reisman told reporters at that time "major issues" remained to be settled before the deadline. On September 14, 1987, the Canadian Prime Minister told provincial premiers that the negotiations were not going well; nine days later the chief Canadian negotiator staged a walkout from the talks. However, on the next day, the 24th, negotiations recommenced at the political level. During the last nine days before the agreement had to be sent to Congress, two Canadian cabinet ministers and the Prime Minister's chief of staff, as well as the United States Trade Representative and the Secretary of the Treasury worked to patch a draft agreement together. The American side also consulted with key congressional leaders. The draft they produced on October 4 required another two months' work by lawyers and trade experts before it could become a legally binding intergovernmental agreement.

More disagreements surfaced during these two months. The U.S. shipping industry wanted shipping to be excluded, and that caused the Canadians to exclude all other kinds of transport. There were changes to the binational panel procedure, including the addition of an appeal panel (*See Chapters 4 and 6 of this book*), and Canada won some protection for cultural industries and crown corporations (nationalized industries). By January 2, 1988, Reagan and Mulroney were able to sign a full agreement, and not just a blank paper which awaited further drafting. (This has happened during some international negotiations.)

A brief summary of some of the most contentious issues, to the extent that they are known, follows. The dispute settlement mechanism was one difficult topic. The Canadians did not want to be subject to either American trade law or American interpretations of that law. They settled for binational interpretation of American law. As for the Autopact, Americans wanted it revised; the Canadians wanted to leave it untouched. In the end, the Canadians agreed to substantive amendments, which, however, left the basic framework in place. Subsidies were controversial; the two governments agreed to postpone their definition to a later date. On intellectual property, another difficult point, the Canadians agreed that Canadian cable companies would pay for American TV programs they picked out of the air, but the issue of patent rights on pharmaceuticals was included in a separate side agreement, so that the Canadians could maintain the fiction of not having made that concession as part of the free trade agreement. On investment, the Canadians conceded to very generous limits, which means that American investment can flow into Canada almost unhindered. At apparently the last minute, the Canadians conceded guaranteed access to their energy resources, and this appears to have been a concession given in return for the dispute settlement procedure. As for the exchange rate of the Canadian dollar, the participants who are still alive insist that it was not included. However, the Canadian dollar rose shortly after the agreement was concluded, and as of mid-1992 was still at that high level.

Other details will perhaps become known as the participants retire to tell their tales. Much of the rest of the story will become known after twenty-five years or so when the two governments open their archives.

Did one side or the other make more concessions? It seems not. Both sides made significant concessions and achieved some of their aims. The review in chapter 5 of the debate in Canada and the United States about this agreement will demonstrate this fact.

The publication, on December 10, 1987, of the final agreement intensified this debate about the desirability of this wide-ranging agreement. Before we turn to that debate, it will be useful to know just what is in the agreement. A brief summary follows.

CHAPTER 4

WHAT IS IT ALL ABOUT?—
SUMMARY OF THE AGREEMENT

INTRODUCTION. The trade agreement[1] which President Reagan and Prime Minister Mulroney signed on January 2, 1988 is about much more than free trade in goods and services. It deals with a large number of topics, from banks to beer, and from government procurement to cable TV. Even though the agreement covers many different topics, it is not as comprehensive an agreement as is that establishing the European Community. The FTA includes large sections of the economy, but skips over others in leapfrog fashion, including a service here, but excluding one there. Except for manufactured goods and some services the FTA is not really about free trade. It is an economic agreement settling many of the questions which have been in dispute between the two countries over the years.

Unlike the European Community treaty, the FTA openly omits political topics. As can be seen from the preamble to the agreement (*See Reading No. 13.*), only two vague clauses include political aims. The first clause mentions "friendship" between the two nations, and the last clause, "broader international cooperation." The seventh clause could also be said to include political aims, in the sense that the idea that "government-created trade distortions" should be reduced, supports a free enterprise ideology that a number of Canadians and even some Americans would also reject.

Dealing as it does with many aspects of a modern economy, the agreement is long and complicated. The English-language version published by the Canadian government is more than

---

[1]The FTA is *not* a treaty, but an agreement between two governments to pass certain legislative measures. It thus did not need a two-thirds majority in the U.S. Senate; instead it passed through the normal legislative procedure in both Houses of Congress and both houses of the Canadian Parliament.

three hundred pages long.[2] A summary of the principal provisions of the agreement follows. In the attempt to simplify, some legal niceties will perhaps be lost.

BEDROCK-FREE TRADE IN GOODS. Before the FTA, over seventy per cent of Canadian-American trade was free of tariffs (though the fact that some goods were tariff free and others were not may in itself have distorted these figures). The FTA removes tariffs on most remaining manufactured goods according to three schedules (chapter 4 of the agreement). The tariffs on about 15 per-cent of goods were eliminated on January 1, 1989; for another 35 per-cent tariffs will be reduced in stages over five years. For the remaining 50 per cent tariffs will be eliminated over a ten year period. This last category includes some articles produced by industries which have long enjoyed considerable protection (furniture, footwear) but also some raw materials, such as lead and zinc ores. The FTA also provides for the gradual elimination of non-tariff barriers, such as quotas, embargoes, and duty remissions.

Because the FTA is a free trade area and not a customs union, it also includes *rules of origin* (chapter 3 of the agreement). Since both Canada and the United States are maintaining their usual customs duties with respect to all other countries, a Mexican manufacturer might, for example, try to ship television parts through the United States to Canada and pass them off as American goods at the Canadian border. To prevent this type of circumvention of the agreement, the FTA says that a good must be transformed sufficiently in either the United States or Canada so as to move from one category on the customs schedule to another. Wood made into furniture, for example, would be reclassified in a different category. But the agreement allows many exceptions to this rule. Textiles, for example, have to be transformed over two categories, that is they need to be changed from thread to fabric to clothing to qualify, whereas in the dairy industry, milk made into cheese is still counted as if it were milk. For some products, there is also a special 50 per cent value

[2]The text of the agreement, entitled *The Canada-U.S. Free Trade Agreement*, is available from the International Communications Group of the Department of External Affairs, 125 Sussex Drive, Ottawa, Canada.

added provision, meaning that the product has to be worth 50 per cent more than it was when it was imported before it can count as a Canadian or American good.

The two governments have also agreed on a common certificate of origin, so that from now on exporters will have to fill out a form explaining how and why the goods fall into the category of Canadian- or American-produced.

To facilitate trade in goods, the FTA provides for *national treatment* and mutual acceptance of inspections and technical standards (chapters 5 and 6). National treatment means that once they enter the United States, Canadian goods are supposed to be treated exactly like American goods with respect to, for example, taxation or safety standards, and American goods are to receive similar treatment in Canada. Learning a lesson from the European Community, which spent many years arguing about how much noise a lawn mower could make before it could be freely traded among member countries, the Canadian and American governments agreed that they would recognize each other's technical standards and the results of testing done in either country. In this way, a lawn mower made in the United States could be sold in Canada if it meets Canadian standards, and a Canadian lawn mower in the United States if it meets American standards.

EXCEPTIONS AND SPECIAL PROVISIONS. The FTA includes special provisions for a large number of individual products (softwood, plywood), but only three large categories of goods are subject to special rules. These are agricultural products, automobiles and parts, and energy.

All industrialized countries subsidize and control agriculture. Under the FTA, the two governments have agreed to be less aggressive in subsidizing agricultural sales to each other or in competition with each other (chapter 7). Canada, for example, will not subsidize most exports to the United States and will buy more American eggs and poultry. The American government has agreed not to impose quotas on Canadian red meat. Canadian horticulture, on the other hand, may be protected for up to twenty years. These are only a few examples out of a complex chapter of the agreement. Also, in agriculture, the two governments will negotiate common standards with respect to, for example, the use of hormones in animal feed or pesticide residues in food. (This constitutes an exception to the rule of national treatment.)

As for wine and liquor, the Canadian government has agreed to reduce the degree of discrimination against American products (chapter 8). Beer is excluded from the FTA. That is, Canada can still protect its beer companies, but the American government reserved the right to deal with beer according to GATT rules. (In 1992, the two governments agreed to free trade in beer by 1993.)

The biggest exception to free trade is in the automotive field (chapter 10). Over 30 per cent of Canadian-American trade consists of automotive products. Since 1965, this trade has been governed by the Autopact, a bilateral agreement which, in effect, guarantees Canada a share of the auto manufacturing industry roughly commensurate with its share of the market. The FTA incorporates the Autopact, but amends it in several ways.

The definition of what constitutes a Canadian or American made vehicle will remain at 50 per cent of the value added, but this 50 per cent will be more strictly defined. In the future, manufacturers will not be able to count overhead and marketing expenses as part of the 50 per cent. Canada has also agreed not to allow any more foreign (that is Asian) car manufacturers to establish themselves in Canada so as to qualify for the Autopact and to phase out duty remission schemes, whereby Canadian manufacturers which export cars can get a refund on duty they have paid on imported parts. In a move that should please Canadian consumers, Canada has lifted the embargo on the importation of second-hand cars. (This writer remembers an incident a few years ago when an American uncle wanted to give his Canadian niece his second-hand Mercedes as a graduation present; there was no legal way this could have been done.) Lastly, the two governments agreed to appoint a "Panel," that is a committee of experts, to study ways in which the Autopact could be further amended and the industry made more competitive as against non-Canadian, non-American (read Japanese) competitors.

There is thus no free trade in automobiles, but an arrangement whereby certain manufacturers have the right to sell their goods within the two countries under specified conditions. This constitutes a kind of managed trade.

In the field of energy, there are also special rules and regulations (chapter 9). The two governments agree to treat each other's energy suppliers as they would domestic producers (national treatment again), but since the energy industry is regulated, this means a considerable degree of government control. The United States cannot in the future impose duties or quotas on Canadian oil, and Canada cannot enforce export prices for oil or gas which are higher than the domestic prices. There are special rules for trade in uranium, and a provision that Canada may buy Alaskan oil. Most important of all, in times of shortage Canada agrees to sell to the United States the same proportion of national production as it did during the previous thirty-six months; this means that if Canada increases its production to allow for, say, a shortfall from the Middle East, it must offer a part of that extra production to U.S. buyers.

Finally, there are a number of exceptions to the rules about trade in goods. Industries can ask to have tariffs eliminated more quickly than is provided for in the FTA (acceleration), or if an industry feels it is in a crisis situation, it can ask to have some of the reductions of tariffs postponed (safeguard measures) (chapter 11).

So overall, the FTA provides for significant but by no means total free trade in goods. Because automobiles and parts, energy, agricultural goods, and softwood lumber are all subject to special rules, the free trade rules on the elimination of duties as such apply to perhaps less than half of Canadian-American trade in goods.

FREE TRADE IN SERVICES. As mentioned in chapter 1 of this book, much of international trade now consists of services. To set an example in the GATT, the two governments intended to liberalize trade in services through the FTA, but by the time each government finished excluding those services it wanted protected, the services chapter (chapter 14) had only limited applicability.

In that chapter, the two governments agree not to impose further restrictions on trade in services in accordance with the principle of national treatment, but this promise applies only to the services listed at the end of chapter 14. All other services are excluded. This means that transport, which the American government did not want to include, and most cultural services, which the Canadian government wanted to exclude, are not covered by the agreement. Most government-provided services, such as health care and education, are also excluded. There is an annex on free trade in architectural services, which was meant to be a model for other service sectors; it, however, is subject to an agreement on common standards by the relevant professional organizations. There are also special provisions for tourism and computer and telecommunications services. The two federal governments also agree to make it somewhat easier for firms from the other country to bid for federal (but not provincial or state) contracts for the supply of goods (but not services) (chapter 13). Defense production is the subject of earlier agreements and is thus also not included in the FTA.

Financial services have their own chapter (chapter 17) and their own rules. Unlike the case of trade in services and goods, this chapter consists of specific but unrelated commitments by each government to allow some of the financial services of the other to operate on its territory. The American government has agreed to allow Canadian banks to sell Canadian government securities in the United States and not to treat Canadian banks less favorably than they were treated in October 1987. The Canadian government has agreed to allow American banks to own a larger share of Canadian banks than they could before the FTA. It will also allow American banks in Canada to expand their holdings and the number of their branches. The agreement does not cover financial institutions regulated by states and provinces (a major exception in the case of the United States).

FREE MOVEMENT OF MONEY AND PEOPLE. Simply put, the FTA provides for the free movement of money, but not of people. Portfolio investment and tourists (with their money) have moved freely across the border since 1948, but the Canadian government has from time to time placed restrictions on direct American investment in Canada (that is U.S. ownership of firms operating in Canada). As of 1974, such investment had to be reviewed by a Canadian government agency, the Foreign Investment Review Agency (FIRA), which the Conservative government later renamed Investment Canada. The FTA limits this kind of Canadian government activity. As of January 1, 1992, only investments worth more than $150 million in 1992 (constant) Canadian dollars will be subject to review. Indirect investments, that is the takeover by one American firm of another American firm which owns a subsidiary in Canada, will not be subject to Canadian government review. Both governments agree to allow profits and dividends to flow freely across the border (Chapter 18.)

Unlike the European Community, the FTA specifically excludes immigration (Chapter 15). There will be no free movement of labor across the border. The FTA does, however, provide for the temporary admission of four categories of people: intra-company transfers, certain professionals who provide a service (for example, a consulting engineer), traders and investors who wish to sell securities in the other country, and a catch-all category called "business visitors," which includes sales personnel and after sales service of goods sold earlier. Persons in all four categories must be Canadian or American citizens.

INSTITUTIONAL PROVISIONS. Table 5 lists all the institutions and committees established under the FTA. The institutions of the FTA are headed by the Commission which is in charge of the over-all administration of the agreement. It consists of the Canadian Minister for International Trade and the U.S. International Trade Representative and is to meet at least once a year. It does not have a staff of its own but relies on a section within the national government departments which these two individuals head. The Commission works by consensus; that is, both sides must agree before a decision is taken. In this way the theoretical legal sovereignty of the two nations is not affected. (Chapter 18.)

Below the Commission there are two kinds of institutions: those which are to implement the agreement as written and those which are to flesh out and extend the FTA by adding details or negotiating on topics not yet covered by the FTA.

The three main implementing institutions consist of the Secretariat, and the Chapter 18 and Chapter 19 panels:

1. Chapter 19 panels constitute a kind of court of appeal

Table 5
List of institutions, committees and similar bodies
existing under the auspices of the FTA as of June 30, 1991
(The numbers in the left margin refer to the relevant
articles of the FTA.)

303	Bilateral Working Group (Rules of Origin and Customs)
705.4	Working Group (to review subsidies on wheat, oats, and barley)
708.4a)	Working Groups on Technical Regulations and Standards for Agricultural Goods

      i) animal health
      ii) plant health, seeds, and fertilizers
      iii) meat and poultry inspection
      iv) dairy, fruit, vegetable, and egg inspection
      v) veterinary drugs and medicated feeds (consisting of five sub-groups)
      vi) food, beverage and colour additives, and unavoidable contaminants
      vii) pesticides
      viii) packaging and labelling of agricultural and related goods
      ix) fish and fishery products*

708.4c)	Joint Monitoring Committee (re. agricultural working groups)
1004	Select Panel on the Automotive Industry
1404	Committee (to set professional standards for architectural and other professional services)
1404, Annex B.4	Tourism Working Group*
1405.2	Working Group on Services*
1503	Working Group on Temporary Entry*
1802	The Commission
1806, 1807	Arbitration Panels
1901.2	Panels to Review Anti-dumping and Countervailing Duty Determination
1903	Panels to Review Statutory Amendments (to national countervail and antisubsidy legislation)
1904.13	Extraordinary Challenge Committee
1907	Working Group (Subsidies and Trade Remedies)

Table 5 (continued)

1908	Binational Working Group (to review functioning of dispute procedures)*
1909	Secretariat
2006.4	Joint Advisory Committee (on transmission rights of television programming)

Letters Appended to the Agreement   Binational Committee on Plywood Standards (created September 1988)

*not provided for in the 1988 Free Trade Agreement but created according to its provisions

Sources: Canada, Department of External Affairs, *The Free Trade Agreement* Ottawa: [1988]; External Affairs and International Trade Canada, *Free Trade News. Implementation and Issues Update*, Ottawa; March 1991; Senate of Canada, *Proceedings of the Senate Committee on Foreign Affairs*; *Free Trade Observer*, May 1990 and Oct. 1990; Mr. James Holbein, Free Trade Secretariat, Department of Commerce, Washington, D.C.

against dumping and countervailing duty decisions by either of the two governments.[3] This is how Chapter 19 panels work: Each government appoints twenty-five experts (usually lawyers) in international trade. When the Canadian or American authorities decide to impose an anti-dumping or countervailing duty, the firm(s) affected have a right to appeal to either the national courts or to a Chapter 19 panel. In the latter case, each government chooses two names (normally from the list of twenty-five names), and the two governments together agree on a fifth name. That panel then deals with the appeal.

Chapter 19 panels constitute an interesting legal innovation, in that they constitute a *binational* review of *national* decisions made according to national legislation.

2. Chapter 18 panels can deal with any kind of dispute about the interpretation of the agreement. It is up to the Commission to

[3]According to one expert, "Dumping is essentially the importation of goods at prices that are lower than domestic prices in the country of export. Countervailable subsidies are certain benefits or payments provided on exports by the government of an exporter. John Kazanjian, "Dispute Settlement Procedures in Canadian Antidumping and Countervailing Duty Cases," in Marc Gold and David Leyton-Brown, eds., *Trade-offs on Free Trade*, Toronto: Carswell, 1988, 198.

appoint a panel when a dispute arises, and it is usually up to the Commission to decide whether or not the decision of the panel will be binding. Like Chapter 19 panels, Chapter 18 panels consist of five persons, who are normally chosen from a pre-existing list, but the Chapter 18 lists are more likely to consist of political personalities than of experts in international trade. (*See Chapter 6 of this book for examples of the work of Chapter 18 and Chapter 19 panels.*)

3. The Secretariat consists of a Canadian section in Ottawa and an American section in Washington. It services the two kinds of panels by, for example, keeping the list of appointees on file, paying the panelists, booking rooms for their meetings, and keeping a file of previous panel decisions for the use of future panels, a task which will obviously expand over the years.

Most of the other groups and committees listed in Table 5 are meant to elaborate on the FTA in some way. The Working Groups on Technical Regulations in Agriculture, for example, are to agree on technical standards in this field. The Working Group on Subsidies and Trade Remedies has seven years to agree on a definition of what constitutes a trade-distorting subsidy.

The FTA includes a large number of provisions for further negotiations of this type, even where there is not a committee to deal with the subject; for example, on government procurement and on services. In this way, the FTA foreshadows further economic cooperation and further common regulation of economic activity between the two partners. The institutions which guide these further negotiations could thus become a source for the growth and expansion of the agreement.

MISCELLANEOUS AND SPECIAL PROVISIONS. The FTA includes a number of other provisions which could lead to further cooperation and harmonization of policies between the two countries. There are, for example, numerous provisions for notification and consultation. The two governments have agreed to notify and/or consult with each other *before* they adopt legislation which could affect the operation of the agreement (clause 1804). In addition, or for greater certainty as a lawyer might say, there are specific instances in which they have agreed to consult; for example, in the case of amendments to anti-dumping legislation. Obviously, this kind of notification is meant to act as a deterrent to legislation which the other partner might consider harmful.

There is another general clause which could expand the scope of the agreement. Under Article 2011, either side may request dispute settlement under Chapter 18 if either government does anything which may cause "nullification or impairment of any benefit reasonably expected . . . directly or indirectly under the provisions of this Agreement." Because the agreement covers so many different areas, this could cause complaints by one government about many different activities of the other government. To use a purely hypothetical example, a Canadian tax on natural gas which made that fuel more expensive in comparison with crude oil might be the subject of a complaint about the benefits reasonably expected from the energy chapter. (Canada exports much more natural gas than oil to the United States.)

Lastly, the FTA became kind of a dumping bin for a number of bilateral commercial disputes which had been irritating the American government for some time. On Canadian cultural policy, for example, the FTA includes a provision that Canadian cable companies will pay royalties on American programs which they pick out of the air and resell to Canadians. Other miscellaneous topics include the elimination of the print-in-Canada requirements for Canadian magazines, the attempt to resolve a dispute about certain grades of plywood, and the folding into the FTA of a 1986 agreement by which Canada agreed to levy an export tax on softwood lumber (though most other export taxes are forbidden under the agreement).

In conclusion, then, this agreement provides for free trade in perhaps half of the trade in goods between the two countries, significantly less in the case of services. Whether an agreement of such scope will have enough momentum to expand into other areas, only time can tell. The story of the first two years of the implementation of the agreement is the subject of chapter 6. First, we will review the national debate in Canada and the discussions in the United States which intervened between the signing and the adoption of the FTA.

CHAPTER 5

FROM SIGNATURE TO IMPLEMENTATION

THE APPROVAL PROCESS. It was almost exactly a year from the time of the signature of the Canada-United States Free Trade Agreement on January 2, 1988, to the time of its coming into force on January 1, 1989. During that year, the Agreement was discussed in several committees of both the U.S. Senate and the House of Representatives, as well as in the two houses as a whole. In the United States, however, there was limited public discussion of the Agreement. In Canada, the year 1988 marked the culmination of a three year long intense public debate. The Canadian government did not ratify the Agreement until after a national election which took on the character of a referendum on the FTA. This chapter is limited to the events of that year, and to a summary of the principal arguments of opponents and supporters of the FTA.

THE UNITED STATES. After the difficulty President Reagan experienced in getting "fast track" negotiating authority from the Congress in April 1986 (see chapter 3 of this book), commentators expected the FTA itself to have an equally rough ride in Congress. This did not happen; it won approval with little opposition. All of the eight House and seven Senate committees which dealt with the FTA reported in its favor. In some of these committees, the vote was either unanimous or unrecorded (a voice vote sufficed).

President Reagan officially submitted the Agreement to Congress on February 9, 1988. Ten days later, Reagan and congressional leaders exchanged letters in which Reagan promised to consult Congress about the necessary implementing legislation, and Congress promised to deal with the FTA before it adjourned for the 1988 elections. Several House and Senate committees began almost immediate hearings on the FTA while bureaucrats, who worked closely with these committees, began to draft the many amendments to American laws that would be needed to implement the Agreement.

The package of implementing legislation was ready July 26, 1988, when Reagan formally submitted it to Congress. As most of the committee hearings had been completed by that date, approval by the two houses was a speedy process. The House of Representatives used only three of the five hours of debating time its leaders had scheduled; on August 9, 1988, it approved the FTA package by a vote of 366 to 40. On September 19, the Senate debated for seven hours, but in the end approved the FTA by an almost identical majority, 83 to 9. Senators do have a reputation for long-windedness. President Reagan signed the legislation on September 28.

A *New York Times* report investigated how the anticipated difficult passage through the complex American legislative process became a cakewalk (Clyde Farnsworth, June 5, 1988). First of all, President Reagan was highly committed to the FTA. A senior American trade official told the author of this book that Reagan would probably consider the FTA to be one of the top five, "perhaps even one of the top three' achievements of his administration. Just why this should be so is not clear, but it may be a combination of the attraction of the word "free" in "free trade," of the idea that something could be done to free rather than restrict trade (this was a time of much protectionist legislation in Congress), as well as of the seduction of Prime Minister Mulroney's flattery.

It followed that administration officials took great care in piloting the legislation through Congress. During the final debate on the FTA, Senator after Senator paid tribute to the administration's efforts to meet the concerns of *his* or *her* state. At congressional request, the implementing legislation included a number of legally ineffective but politically satisfying provisions. Thus, the President promised to monitor Canadian subsidies, to begin negotiations about Canadian potato imports, and to study Canadian restrictions on imports of unprocessed fish. Congress authorized the President to negotiate higher North American content requirements under the Autopact. The administration also agreed to some legislative amendments in order to please wavering Congressmen. There was a slight tightening of the regulations governing the import of wheat, and a promise not to lower tariffs on plywood until Canada and the United States agreed to common standards. (As of April 1992, there was no agreement on such standards.) The President also agreed not to implement the American legislation until the Canadian legislation was in place.

Finally, and most important of all, is the fact that the FTA is highly favorable to American interests. Those who thought they might be adversely affected were few, far between, and for the most part, politically ineffective. (See the section on Proponents and Opponents, later in this chapter.)

Canada. In Canada, the Free Trade Agreement became the center of an emotionally charged political debate. Prime Minister Mulroney had a majority in the House of Commons, and in spite of delaying tactics and displays, such as the waving of flags and the singing of the national anthem by opposition members, he was able to have the implementing legislation adopted on August 31, 1988, by a vote of 177 to 64. But the opposition Liberal Party controlled the (appointed) Senate, and they refused to adopt the legislation unless Mulroney first called a general election. Mulroney did so, on October 1. The election was held on November 21, 1988.

In Canada, free trade with the United States had been the subject of an intense national debate since 1985. Dozens of books and conferences and thousands of newspaper and magazine articles debated the pros and cons of a free trade agreement with the United States. Most of the participants now threw their energy into the seven week election campaign. It came to a dramatic climax on October 25, when Mulroney faced the leader of the opposition Liberal party, John Turner, in a televised debate. Turner made a strong appeal to Canadian nationalism, and bested Mulroney in the English as well as in the (earlier) French language debate. Until then the opinion polls had been indecisive, but for a few days after the debate, they changed (*See Figure 1.*) The Liberals gained ground. But Turner's disorganized and underfinanced Liberal Party lacked credibility with the voters. Many of those who opposed the Free Trade Agreement chose to vote for the other opposition party, the New Democratic Party (NDP). On election day, 32 per cent of Canadians voted for the Liberals, 20 per cent for the NDP, and 43 per cent for Mulroney's Conservatives. If the election had been a referendum on the FTA, the Agreement would have lost, but under the single member constituency system which both

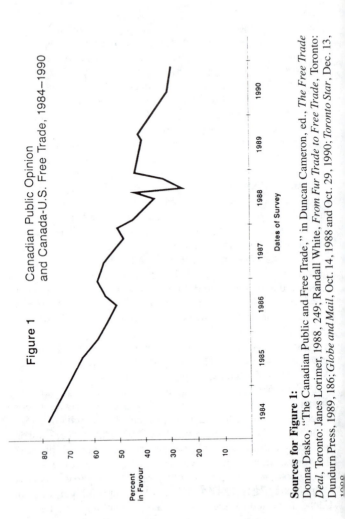

Figure 1

Canadian Public Opinion
and Canada-U.S. Free Trade, 1984–1990

Sources for Figure 1:
Donna Dasko, "The Canadian Public and Free Trade," in Duncan Cameron, ed., *The Free Trade Deal*, Toronto: Janes Lorimer, 1988, 249; Randall White, *From Fur Trade to Free Trade*, Toronto: Dundurn Press, 1989, 186; *Globe and Mail*, Oct. 14, 1988 and Oct. 29, 1990; *Toronto Star*, Dec. 13, 1989.

Canada and the United States use to elect the lower house of their legislature, the results gave Mulroney a majority of 169 out of a total 295 members of parliament.

After another heated debate and further displays of emotion and patriotism, the Canadian House of Commons adopted the FTA implementing legislation in the early hours of December 24, 1988. The Senate did so six days later, on December 30. In accordance with its pre-election promise, the Liberal majority abstained, allowing the Conservatives to pass the legislation. Later that day, in the absence of the Governor-General, a supreme court justice signed the package of legislation into law.

PROPONENTS AND OPPONENTS. The United States. Among those who were aware of it, the FTA had widespread support in the United States. The Ways and Means Committee of the U.S. House of Representatives held six days of hearings on the FTA, and even in this forum, where one might have expected any opponents to come forward, there were relatively few to speak against it.

The business community gave the FTA overwhelming support. The American Coalition for Trade Expansion with Canada, a lobby group formed in support of the FTA, claimed a membership of 530 firms and submitted a list to prove it. The list included practically every major corporation in the United States, from AT&T to General Dynamics, General Electric, General Motors, and Upjohn Company. The few business groups who spoke against the agreement included some independent petroleum producers, automotive parts producers, and firms which mined zinc and uranium. Agricultural interests, with the exception of potato growers and some fishing interests, gave the FTA lukewarm support. State governments also supported the Agreement; the National Governors' Association voted for it, 30 to 5. (Not all the governors attended that day.) All of the major newspapers supported the FTA; *The New York Times*, *The Washington Post*, the *Los Angeles Times*, the *Chicago Tribune*, and the *Wall Street Journal* gave it strong editorial endorsement.

Apart from the few industrial groups mentioned, the only significant opposition to the FTA came from the labor movement. The AFL-CIO, the Teamsters Union, and the UAW all spoke against the Agreement as did textile manufacturers and workers.

There was no clear cut political division among supporters and opponents; Republicans and Democrats could be found in both camps. Geographically, opponents were most likely to be among the resource producers of the Northwest, in New England (especially Maine), and in New Mexico (which produces uranium).

Canada. Canadians were more divided than were Americans on the issue of the FTA. Historically, business, especially manufacturing and the large banks, had opposed free trade with the United States, but in 1987 and 1988 they were all strong supporters of the FTA. The difference this time lay in the fact that many of the major Canadian firms were either subsidiaries of American firms or had other types of corporate links with major American groups. As for the banks, Canadian banks, which enjoy a more favorable legal infrastructure than do their American counterparts, hoped to do good business in the United States.

As in the United States, the Canadian business community joined together in a lobby group in support of the Agreement; in Canada, this group was known as the Canadian Alliance for Trade and Job Opportunities. Surveys of large corporations and of small and medium-sized businesses showed overwhelming business support for the FTA.[1]

Most of the press and the major periodicals supported the FTA. The mass circulation *Toronto Star* was the only consistent opponent in this field, although the *Montreal Gazette* carried a series of anti-FTA cartoons. Nationally, the FTA had the support of only one of the three major political parties, the Conservatives. However, eight of the ten provincial governments, including the Liberal government of Quebec, supported the FTA. The western provinces, which are exporters of resources and semi-processed goods, were especially strong supporters.

Canadian opponents to the FTA formed an umbrella organization, The Coalition Against Free Trade (which later became

[1] Alan Rugman, "The Free Trade Agreement and the Global Economy," *Business Quarterly*, Summer 1988, no pagination.

the Pro-Canada Network). In addition, a group which consisted of individual members was formed to oppose free trade. This group, the Council of Canadians, in turn joined the Coalition Against Free Trade along with the many other groups who opposed the FTA.

These opponents included practically all of the labor movement as well as most of the cultural community, that is writers and artists. The Liberal Party and the social democratic NDP opposed the Agreement, as did the Liberal government of Ontario. Agriculture was divided; fruit and vegetable growers were most concerned about American competition; meat producers were strongly in favor. Several representatives of the two major Canadian churches, the Roman Catholic and the United Church, also spoke out against the FTA. Academics, with the exception of those who taught commerce or economics, tended to be opposed. Women's groups, environmentalists, and peace groups also opposed the FTA since they all perceived the American political culture as less sympathetic to their causes than the Canadian one. Then there were individual efforts, such as the man who drove his old red pick-up truck across the country selling anti-free trade T-shirts, or the retired family court judge, Marjorie Bowker, who wrote a book against the Agreement. (*See note 9 later in this chapter.*)

As the previous paragraph demonstrates, in Canada support or opposition to the FTA followed ideological lines. Most of those who are considered at the center or the Left of the Canadian political spectrum opposed the Agreement; those on the Right supported it. That helps to explain the opposition of the Liberal governments in Ontario and Prince Edward Island, and the support of the more Right-wing Liberal government in Quebec (though in Quebec support for the FTA was strong, even among some normally Left-wing groups).

Public Opinion. Between April 1984 and late 1990, at least thirty Canadian public opinion polls asked about the Canada-United States free trade issue. Figure 1 summarizes the polls which simply asked whether the respondent was for or against free trade with the United States, or was for or against the agreement signed in 1988. The graph shows a pattern: widespread support in 1984 and 1985, a gradual decrease in that support until it reached a low point at the height of the 1988 election campaign, then an increase to moderate support levels, with a renewed decline as the 1990 recession began to take hold.

Since the 1850s, it has been a truism of Canadian history that Canadians turn to the United States when times get tough. An independent economy is a luxury for good times. In 1911, one of the arguments used against free trade with the United States was that Canada was prosperous and did not need free trade at that time. During the Depression, Canadians once again turned to trade agreements with the United States, and because the agreements were concluded at a time when the worst of the Depression was already over, the magic formula—better trade relations with the United States equals prosperity—seemed once again to work. Interest in free trade revived during the recession of 1982, but this time the historic formula has let Canadians down. By the time the FTA was negotiated and in place, the business cycle had completed another turn, and North America was once again in recession. Now that Canadians have both recession *and* a free trade agreement with the United States, many of them have turned against the latter.

Not included in Figure 1 are the *Maclean's* polls which asked about "the idea" of free trade. These polls showed a much higher level of support than did the more specific question; in November 1988, for example, 57 per cent favored the idea of free trade, but only 26 to 34 per cent favored free trade! (There were many polls that month.)

In the United States, there seem to have been no public opinion polls on this issue at that time. One was held in 1990, when free trade with Mexico became an issue. That poll showed Americans equally split with 35 per cent in favor and 35 per cent opposed.[2]

THE DEBATE ABOUT FREE TRADE. A principle first identified by Barbara Haskel of McGill University states that during international negotiations, the more powerful partner will stress the general good to be derived from a successful agreement, whereas the weaker partner will try to make sure

[2]*Maclean's*, June 25, 1990, 64.

that as many details as possible are covered by the agreement. It is perhaps an elaboration of this principle, that American proponents of the FTA tended to stress its general, political, and world-wide benefits, whereas Canadian proponents tried to identify the specific benefits for the Canadian economy. The converse was also true. American opponents of the FTA stressed its specific disadvantages for some industries, groups, or regions, whereas Canadian opponents tended to speak in general terms about the dangers to Canada's future.

American Arguments for the FTA. American proponents of the Agreement mentioned the political advantages of working with an ally, but most of their political arguments related to the domestic politics of the two countries. The FTA was seen to undercut the position of the protectionists in Congress, and in Canada, to make it difficult for future governments to introduce nationalist measures of the type used by Trudeau and his governments.

Most of the arguments used by the American proponents of the FTA consisted of a combination of the political and the economic. They pointed to the advantages of liberalizing trade with the United States' major trading partner, of the good example this agreement would set for the multilateral negotiations, and failing that, the fact that such an agreement would demonstrate to unyielding negotiating partners that the United States has alternatives to multilateral trade agreements. There were also frequent references to the possible extension of this or a similar agreement to other countries such as Mexico. (*See Reading No. 14.*) The fact that the FTA would give the United States assured access to Canada's energy resources was another argument which is both political and economic in nature.

On purely economic grounds, American proponents pointed out that bilateral free trade would strengthen the competitive position of the industries of both nations by forcing them to become more efficient (or go out of business). They hoped that such strengthened industries would be able to compete more successfully than they had in the past in markets in other parts of the world. There seem to have been few studies of the precise economic effect the FTA might have on the U.S. economy, though the ITC studied possible effects on some specific industries. One Canadian study predicted gains of $600 million, or .03 per cent of GNP.[3] This may have been the same study Congressmen DeLay (from Texas) was referring to when he stated during the debate in the House of Representatives (August 9, 1988) that he had heard the FTA would lead to the creation of 500,000 to 750,000 jobs in the United States.

U.S. proponents also identified specific advantages of the FTA. These included revisions to the Autopact, assured access to Canada for U.S. investment, the removal of Canadian tariffs, which are higher than the American, access to the Canadian market for some agricultural goods, and royalty payments for cable television signals. (*See Reading No. 15.*)

American Arguments Against the FTA. American opponents to the FTA consisted of two major groups, and each group had a specific type of argument against the FTA. Senators and Congressmen who opposed the agreement argued in terms of the specific industries which would be affected by the FTA. The industries mentioned included fishing in general, lobster fishing, potatoes, domestic oil production, and lead, zinc and uranium mining. The usual argument was that the equivalent Canadian industries were subsidized by the Canadian government; that is why the U.S. industries could not compete. (*See Reading No. 16.*) The word "unfair" was the one opponents frequently used with respect to so-called Canadian subsidies. The exemption for Canada's cultural industries was also widely criticized.

During the hearings held by the House Ways and Means Committee, the AFL-CIO, the United Auto Workers, and the Teamsters Union all testified against the FTA. While the Auto Workers and the Teamsters complained of specific negative effects on the auto industry and trucking (the Canadian market was said to be closed to American trucking), the AFL-CIO feared that the agreements supposed emphasis on services

[3]Richard Lipsey and Murray Smith, "The Canada-U.S. Free Trade Agreement: Special Case or Wave of the Future," in Jeffrey Schott, ed., *Free Trade Areas and U.S. Trade Policy*, Washington: Institute for International Economics, 1989, 319.

meant that the United States had given up on its manufacturing industry. They also objected to the "grandfathering" of a number of Canadian practices, such as protection for provincial beer industries, and the fact that Canadian tariffs would stay high for a number of years. The AFL-CIO also feared that the agreement was but a step on the way to an agreement with Mexico (*See Reading No. 17.*). The UAW objected to the 50 per cent North American content requirement for cars, which they considered to be too low, and the Canadian incentives to Japanese and Korean car manufacturers who were building plants in Canada (the so-called transplants).

U.S. opponents had one general argument against the FTA. They objected to the binational panels which they saw as an erosion of U.S. sovereignty. They especially feared that the panels would take away Congress's ability to protect U.S. industry, and that they might become examples for other arrangements of a similar nature. The labor opponents used one other argument. They pointed out that they were acting in solidarity with their Canadian counterparts, and the Teamsters, not generally known for left-wing rhetoric, accused the Reagan administration of "a crude attempt . . . to preserve an allied conservative government in a neighboring country."[4]

Canadian Arguments for the FTA. For the most part, Canadian proponents of the FTA tried to be precise and specific in their arguments in support of the deal. A number of economists studied the possible economic effects of free trade with the United States and later of the specific Agreement negotiated. Most of these studies predicted considerable gains for the Canadian economy. A Canadian Department of Finance summary of some of these studies showed that the minimum gain predicted was one of 0.7 per cent rise in "real income"; the maximum, a whopping 8.9 per cent; most estimates were in the 2 to 3 per cent range. The summary also claimed that benefits would accord to all regions of Canada and to most industrial sectors. The OECD, in its annual survey of the Canadian

[4]Paul R. Locigno to the Subcommittee on Trade of the Committee on Ways and Means Committee of the House of Representatives, Feb. 26, 1988, p. 171. (Serial 100–59)

economy, predicted "large economic benefits" from the FTA, but did not mention a specific figure.[5]

Some economists tried to convert these gains in income into estimates of the number of jobs that might be created. They predicted the creation of as many as 350,000 jobs during the phasing in of the Agreement, and they even claimed that as many as 120,000 jobs might be created in the first four years.[6]

Other economists were more careful. Richard Harris pointed out that the estimates would not hold if there was a recession; in any case, he wrote, there might not be more jobs but that those that remained were likely to be higher paying jobs. If, as economists were predicting, the force of competition would make the Canadian economy more efficient, this would mean a rise in productivity and thus higher incomes for those who had jobs, especially those with specialized skills.[7] It would also mean that less efficient producers might go out of business, so that some jobs would be lost. Economists also wrote of the benefits of longer production runs and greater specialization.

These benefits as well as increased competition and imports of lower priced American goods were expected to lead to lower prices for Canadian consumers. One commentator even claimed to have calculated how much a family would save on groceries or furniture. (*See Reading No. 19.*) Proponents also promised benefits from increased American investment, investment which was expected both because Canadian investment controls had been lifted and because firms investing in Canada would have guaranteed access to the U.S. market.

Canadian supporters of the FTA also made a number of defensive arguments. They pointed out that the FTA would shelter Canada from U.S. protectionism, and that the multilateral trade system, on which Canada had relied since World War II, was not working as it used to. They pointed to the creation of regional trading blocs and claimed that Canada also needed assured access to a large market. (*See Reading No. 18.*)

[5]Canada, Department of Finance, *The Canada-U.S. Free Trade Agreement: An Economic Assessment*, Ottawa: [1988], 32–34; *Globe and Mail*, September 17, 1988.

[6]Canada, Department of Finance, 37–38.

[7]Richard Harris, "Employment Effects," in Crispo, John, ed., *Free Trade. The Real Story*, Toronto: Gage, 1988, 111 and 115.

Government spokespersons were especially proud of the dispute settlement procedure, which they claimed would protect Canadian exports from the harassment of U.S. agencies which were trying to protect various U.S. industries.

Other defensive arguments tried to refute the claims made by the FTA's opponents. Government and business supporters of the FTA insisted that the Agreement protected Canadian culture and Canadian sovereignty. They pointed out that Canada still had the right to limit imports on the basis of health or security concerns, and that there was no mention in the Agreement of social or regional development policies. Only occasionally did a supporter of the Agreement mention that it also would have the effect of tying the hands of future Canadian governments, so that if a government wanted to limit foreign investment or implement a national energy policy it would have to abrogate an international agreement first. Sometimes, supporters also pointed out that the FTA might force the provinces to lower or abolish inter-provincial barriers to trade. In these two respects, proponents presented the FTA as a means of affecting domestic policy.

It is ironic that when some U.S. opponents of the FTA presented the Agreement as a threat to U.S. sovereignty, some Canadian proponents of the FTA wanted just such a reduction in sovereignty so as to reduce the freedom of action of future federal and provincial governments. Peter Lougheed, a former premier of Alberta, rejoiced in the fact that the FTA would prevent future Canadian governments from introducing any kind of national energy policy.

In general, the Canadian supporters of the FTA tried to present themselves as rational, cool headed analysts. They saw the opponents of the FTA as being excessively emotional; the FTA's supporters gave their publications titles such as *Free Trade. The Real Story* (*See note 7, above*) or "Straight Talk on Free Trade" (*See Reading No. 19.*) or *The Canada-U.S. Free Trade Agreement: an Economic Assessment* (*See Note 5, above*). They referred to chapters or articles of the Agreement, and when they spoke of its overall effects, they tended to refer to specific economic studies. There was, nevertheless, a certain hysteria in their determination to have the agreement adopted. As one observer put it, the FTA's Canadian supporters seemed to think that the sky would fall in if the Agreement was not adopted.[8]

They also accused the FTA's opponents of lacking faith in Canadians and their ability to compete in the U.S. market. They painted a picture of a strong, prosperous Canada as a part of a strong prosperous North America (*See Reading No. 20a.*).

Canadian Arguments Against the FTA. Canadian opponents of the FTA concentrated on what they believed would be the over-all effects of the implementation of the Agreement. They were frequently emotional in their appeal to Canadian nationalism, and what is more, were proud of this fact (*See Reading No. 21.*). The title of some of their writings indicates this: *If You Love this Country: Facts and Feelings on Free Trade*, *On Guard for Thee*, (which is a line from the national anthem), or "Surrendering National Sovereignty."[9] The main anti-FTA lobbying group simply called itself the "Council of Canadians," as if to call themselves Canadian was a sufficient indication of their position.

Several years later, it is hard to recreate the emotional intensity of this debate. A couple of incidents may help to do this. In the medium sized city of Sudbury, Ontario, one of many groups across the country which had lobbied against capital punishment was called the Sudbury and District Anti-Capital Punishment Coalition. After the Canadian House of Commons abolished capital punishment (on June 30, 1988), this group, with but few changes of personnel, became the Sudbury and District Anti-Free Trade Coalition. This is not to suggest that anyone thought that free trade would lead to the introduction of capital punishment in Canada, but it shows that the opponents of the FTA had a vision of their country as a peaceful, non-violent society; they saw the FTA as a threat to the realization of that vision. (See Cartoon 1.)

---

[8]William Watson, "The Draft Agreement: Cohabitation Worth a Try," in A.R. Riggs and Tom Welk, eds., *Canadian-American Free Trade: (The Sequel)*, Halifax: Institute for Research on Public Policy, 1988, 58.

[9]Laurier LaPierre, ed., *If You Love this Country. Facts and Feelings on Free Trade*, Toronto: McClelland and Stewart, 1988; Marjorie Montgomery Bowker, *On Guard for Thee*, Hull: Voyageur Publishing, 1988; Canadian Labour Congress, "Surrendering National Sovereignty," in Duncan Cameron, ed., *The Free Trade Papers*, Toronto: James Lorimer, 1986, 135–142.

Reproduced by permission. Star Syndicate, Toronto. A Canadian cartoonist's view of the consequences of the FTA.

The second incident consists of an event organized by the nation-wide Coalition Against Free Trade. On November 25, 1988, the Coalition hired one of the major concert halls in downtown Toronto. There artists, musicians, and actors read from their work, sang songs and performed skits about Canada and against free trade. There was a large turnout, and the emotional intensity and conviction of that evening swept along many a waverer.

The Canadian opponents of the FTA saw their country as a caring, peaceful, and environmentally responsible community. They believed that these attributes were not those of the United States, and that the FTA was an attempt to make Canada and Canadians more like the United States and Americans. They claimed that Canada's social programs, such as health care and unemployment insurance, might be defined as unfair subsidies, and that the supporters of the FTA might use the Agreement to attack those social programs so as to reduce taxes on corporations and wealthy Canadians. They also pointed to the important role that government has traditionally played in the Canadian economy, and they feared that the FTA was meant to reduce the role of the state to that which it is in the United States. (*See Reading No. 22.*) Though most of them had never heard of the functional theory of integration (*See Chapter 1 of this book*), the FTA's opponents felt that somehow economic integration would lead to political integration.

The FTA's opponents claimed that the Agreement might reduce Canada's ability to follow an independent foreign policy. If Canada became more closely tied to the American economy, it would not be able to oppose U.S. foreign policy in other areas, such as Latin America or the Middle East; the American government would be able to use economic pressure to silence a critical Canada. They also pointed out the advantages a middle power such as Canada can derive from facing a superpower in a multilateral forum, where it has the support of others, as against a bilateral forum, where it is automatically outgunned (figuratively speaking)!

Some of the Canadian opponents of the FTA believed that the pressure of American competition would force Canada to lower its environmental standards with respect to, for example, acid rain causing emissions. They saw the United States as technology-driven and unresponsive to environmental considerations whereas Canadians were somehow closer to nature.

The second main theme of the Canadian FTA opponents was the loss of Canadian control over resources and other aspects of the economy. (*See Reading No. 20c.*). They pointed out that the FTA gave the United States guaranteed access to Canada's energy resources. American firms were guaranteed the right to invest in Canada and would face review of only a few of the largest investments (over $150 million in constant 1992 Canadian dollars). In spite of the exclusion of Canada's cultural industries, any future changes in any Canadian policy, cultural or otherwise, would be subject to U.S. retaliation because the two national governments reserved the right to retaliate if either moved to nullify any of the benefits of the FTA. In general, the Canadian opponents of the Agreement claimed that the government, in its anxiety to score a success, had given away far more than it had received. *(See Cartoon 2).*

Some of the Canadian critics of the FTA tried to be specific in their comments. This was especially true of the political opposition and of one of the FTA's most lucid critics, Lloyd Axworthy, a Liberal member of parliament. *(See Reading No. 22.)* Some of these more specific criticisms included predictions of the loss of tens of thousands of jobs, particularly in the manufacturing

Reproduced by permission, Krieger, Vancouver, Canada. A Canadian cartoonist's view of the free trade negotiations.

industries of southern Ontario and Quebec. Without tariffs U.S. multinationals would have few reasons to invest in Canada because they could simply supply the Canadian market from U.S. plants. The Canadian Autoworkers Union claimed that the Autopact provisions guaranteeing a proportion of production in Canada had been emasculated. Other Canadian critics pointed out that the government's vaunted dispute settlement procedure did not give Canada any exemption from American protectionist legislation, but simply meant that a binational panel would interpret American law as it applied to the exports of Canadian firms (*See Reading No. 20b.*)

Two economists tackled the logic of the FTA's supporters head-on. While it is not possible to summarize all of their complex economic reasoning, the main elements were these: Removal of Canada's tariffs will cause some Canadian firms to go out of business or cut employment. These firms will not be able to invest more so as to cut production costs and become more efficient. Removal of the American tariff is supposed to give Canadian firms access to a larger market, but Americans may find other ways to protect their industries. In any case, Canadian firms which are under pressure to reduce costs and have little government assistance, will not be able to take advantage of the American market.[10] To this argument, the Canadian UAW (it soon became the CAW) added that a large home market had not helped American firms to compete against Japanese and Korean companies.

CONCLUDING REMARKS. In the United States, the FTA had overwhelming support. Critics knew that they were only defending a few special interests, and as such they were highly defensive or guarded in their comments. There were few if any ringing denunciations. The fact was that the FTA was favorable to most American interests.

The story was very different in Canada where the jobs and futures of many Canadians, and perhaps the existence of Canada, not as a separate country, but as a distinct society and

[10]Kieran Furlong and Douglas Moggach, "Efficiency, Competition and Full Employment in Canadian Free Trade Literature," *Studies in Political Economy*, vol. 33 (Autumn 1990), 135–156.

political culture were at stake. The debate in Canada dealt with basic economic and political questions. Does greater economic integration lead to greater political integration? Is it rational to place economic over other kinds of values, or is there another kind of rationality? What does it mean to be Canadian? Is nationalism a worthwhile value still?

In the end, the Canadian opponents of the FTA, although they seem to have had a slim majority of Canadians on their side, were probably just a little too emotional in their argumentation. One cannot but feel for them. They fought against big money; the Alliance for Trade and Job Opportunities spent $2 million on the campaign for the FTA, the Pro-Canada Network, $750,000 on the campaign against.[11] They also had to argue against important people, and they lost out to cold economic logic and apparent rational economic advantage. And they were haunted by the fact that, as the *Maclean's* polls mentioned above show, most Canadians and Americans do believe in free trade and a free economy. The question was one of the degree and kind of governmental and societal control.

Most of the predictions of the Canadian supporters of the FTA have already been proved wrong. (*See Chapter 7 of this book.*) A longer time period will be needed to show if the opponents were right in their predictions.

---

[11] Janet Hiebert, "Fair Elections and Freedom of Expression under the Charter," *Journal of Canadian Studies* 24:4 (Winter 1989–90), 80.

CHAPTER 6

THE IMPLEMENTATION OF
THE AGREEMENT

INTRODUCTION. By July 1991, the FTA had been in force for two and a half years. For a trade agreement, that is a very short time. It took the European Community four years to agree on its first significant new program (the Common Agricultural Policy negotiated in 1962). Similarly, it may take some years before some of the provisions of the FTA are implemented.

This chapter reviews the implementation of the FTA in accordance with the summary of the agreement given in chapter 4.[1] (*Readings Nos. 23 and 24* summarize the views of the two governments on the second anniversary of the FTA.) As we survey the various implementation measures, the reader should keep in mind that the commitments made in the FTA are of two kinds. First, there are provisions to take specific action within specified time periods, such as the requirement that tariffs be lowered by a fixed percentage point, that Canada be allowed to buy Alaskan oil or that the Canadian National Energy Board change the means by which it calculates minimum export prices. Second, there are agreements to agree, or so-called framework provisions. Under these the two governments agree to negotiate further sub-agreements at a later date (for example, to further liberalize trade in services) or to take further actions at an unspecified time (for example, to recognize product testing done in each other's standards testing laboratories).

FREE TRADE IN GOODS. The removal of tariffs has not only proceeded on schedule; some tariffs are actually being

[1]This chapter is for the most part based on the following two documents: *The United States-Canada Free-Trade Agreement. Biennial Report*. A Report from the President to the Congress under Section 304(f) of the United States-Canada Free Trade Agreement, [Washington]: Jan. 1991, and External Affairs and International Trade Canada, *Free Trade News. Implementation and Issues Update*. Ottawa: March 1991. Officials from both governments read an earlier draft of the chapter and suggested revisions.

removed more quickly than foreseen. Under a procedure for the accelerated reduction of tariffs, the two governments, after extensive consultation with their industries, agreed that tariffs on over four hundred items would be reduced ahead of schedule on April 1, 1990. A second set of accelerated tariff reductions, affecting another four hundred tariff items, came into force on July 1, 1991. Neither government has made use of the safeguard provisions by which it could have the reduction of some tariffs postponed.

The mutual recognition of standards has made less progress. As of June 1991, neither government had licensed any laboratory in the other country for the purpose of testing goods which are to be traded. The American Congress has, however, exempted Canada from new non-tariff protective measures it has imposed. In 1990, for example, Congress instituted new inspection standards for industrial steel fasteners (U.S. Fastener Quality Act), claiming that Third World countries were sending substandard fasteners to the United States. Congress exempted Canada from this legislation.

Special Provisions re Trade in Goods. Most of the provisions with respect to agriculture have been carried out to the extent that they involved specific commitments, such as a commitment not to subsidize sales to each other or the commitment by the provincial governments not to charge discriminatory prices on American whisky, but there have also been some failures in this area.

The provisions whereby the United States agreed to accept meat inspected by Canadian meat inspectors has been implemented partly, so that some Canadian meat is still inspected twice, once in Canada and once in the United States. The clause whereby Canada can seasonally protect its fruit and vegetable growers failed its first test in the spring of 1990 when Canadian bureaucrats miscalculated the possible duties on asparagus. The eight committees which are to agree on common standards on everything from veterinary medicines to pesticides are busily at work and a ninth committee, on fish products, has been added. There are, however, few agreements as yet. As of 1989, the Canadian Wheat Board will no longer require licenses for the importation of U.S. oats and oat products; U.S. wheat and barley, however, still required such licenses until May 1991, when an increase in the subsidies the Canadian government pays to its wheat farmers brought into force a provision of the FTA which allows American wheat into Canada when the subsidies Canadian farmers receive are higher than those paid to American farmers. This was the first time in forty-eight years that American wheat was allowed into Canada. Canada has also accused the United States of not adhering to a commitment, included in the FTA, not to subsidize further exports in the other partner's traditional markets. In February 1991, Canada's Minister of Agriculture said that the United States had subsidized over 80 percent of the price of a wheat sale to Norway.[2]

The Autopact has been amended in accordance with the FTA. The Automotive Select Panel has met several times and has commissioned two studies. One study recommends increasing the Canadian/American value-added for qualifying vehicles to 60 per cent from the current 50 per cent. The Canadian government has refused to consider this recommendation, which is also opposed by General Motors and the Japanese and Korean "transplants" who manufacture cars in Canada; it is supported by the U.S. government and by Chrysler and Ford. The other study, on the global competitiveness of the North American auto industry, has just been completed. The attempt to flesh out the Autopact provisions of the FTA has since been overtaken by the free trade negotiations with Mexico. (*See chapter 7 of this book*.)

The provisions of the energy chapter of the FTA have been carried out. Canada's National Energy Board has changed the way in which it calculates the permissible prices for licensed exports, and Canada has begun to sell unprocessed uranium to the United States. The real test for the energy chapter could come at a time of shortage, something which in spite of the Persian Gulf Crisis of 1990–91 has not yet happened.

FREER TRADE IN SERVICES. The services chapter included no immediate commitments and can be said to have worked to the extent that the governments have placed no further restrictions on trade in services. The provision whereby the two governments are to negotiate further liberalization of trade in

[2]*Globe and Mail*, Feb. 6, 1991.

services has not led to any new agreements. The model agreement on architecture, which was appended to the chapter on services, has not yet been carried out because the professional associations have not been able to agree on the definition of a qualified architect.

With respect to financial services, both governments have amended their national legislation, as provided for in the agreement. Americans are exempt from the foreign ownership requirements to which Canadian law subjects other foreign banks and can operate in Canada in competition with Canadian banks. American Express was the first U.S. bank to take advantage of this freedom. Canadian banks have been active in the United States for some time and are now guaranteed the legal right to continue to do so.

FREE MOVEMENT OF MONEY AND PEOPLE. Canada has carried out the changes to its foreign investment review legislation as required by the FTA. The amount that an American firm can spend to buy a Canadian one before being subject to a review by a Canadian government agency is to reach $150 million in constant Canadian dollars by January 1, 1993. There seem to have been no complaints from either side about lack of national treatment[3] in this field.

The limited provisions for the movement of temporary workers across the border have been successfully implemented. One measure of their success is the fact that the list of eligible professions has been amended several times. Journalists have been removed from the list, bus and coach drivers and geochemists are among those who are to be added. Minimum qualifications have been established for several of the listed professions.

During 1989, 18,782 Canadians crossed to the United States, and 2,760 Americans came to Canada under the temporary entry provisions. These figures, however, do not include salespersons, after sales service representatives and invited speakers (a category collectively known as business visitors). The Canadian government believes that the total number in this category

[3]"National treatment" means that firms registered or owned in another country should be given the same rights and privileges as firms registered or owned in the host country.

is probably greater than that in the other three combined. (The figures in this paragraph were provided by an official in the Canadian Department of External Affairs; the figures given in the U.S. President's biennial review are somewhat lower.)

A movement of people that the drafters of the FTA did not foresee is that of Canadians who flock across the border to do their shopping. Every weekend thousands do so, and a report by Canada's Senate claims that American shopping centers have been built near the border to attract Canadian shoppers. The same report says that half the population of Canada's Niagara region shops in the United States from time to time and that the people in this region alone spend C$115 million a year on such shopping.

This unforeseen development illustrates the psychological effect an international agreement can have. If controlled by Canadian customs, much of this shopping would be illegal under the FTA. Textiles, for example, are subject to special rules, as are agricultural products (groceries). Many other purchases, such as Japanese made computers or Mexican assembled television sets would fail to qualify under the rules of origin. Canadians have chosen to believe that "free trade" means what it says, and the Canadian authorities have preferred not to enforce some provisions of the FTA.

THE INSTITUTIONS OF THE FTA. As pointed out in chapter 4, all of the institutions provided for in the treaty have been established, as have several new ones. (*See Table 5 in Chapter 4.*) The principal institutions also seem to be functioning as intended.

As of April 1992, twenty-three Chapter 19 panels had been appointed to review nineteen cases. Twelve of these panels were constituted because Canadians wished to appeal the decision of American trade authorities; the other two because Americans sought to appeal the decisions of Canadian authorities. There have been many more American than Canadian chapter 19 cases because Canadian authorities have been successful in making informal arrangements with American importers (so called "undertakings") which result in the settling of the dispute. Most of the chapter 19 cases have dealt with specialized products, little known to the general public. Thus, there was one about the sale of red raspberries from British Columbia, and another about replacement parts for paving equipment.

A panel which has dealt with a larger category of goods, that of the sale of Canadian pork to the United States, is the one which has been the most controversial. The U.S. Commerce Department found that Canadian subsidies to the pork industry were countervailable, and the International Trade Commission (ITC) found a threat of material injury to the U.S. pork industry. The Canadian pork exporting industry requested binational panel reviews of both findings.

The panel dealing with the threat of injury findings has focused attention on the details of the binational dispute resolution procedure. This panel remanded, or referred, decisions back to the ITC two times. The first remand decisions found that the ITC had used "questionable" statistics and directed it to recalculate its results. The ITC confirmed its original findings, and the Canadian industry reconvened the panel a second time. In January 1991, the panel again remanded to the ITC, instructing it to use only certain types of data. This time (February 1991), the ITC found that there had **not** been material injury to the U.S. industry.

The U.S. pork producing industry then requested that the U.S. government invoke the "Extraordinary Challenge" provisions of the FTA. On March 29, 1991, Carla Hills, the U.S. Trade Representative, requested the convening of an Extraordinary Challenge Committee, alleging that the latest panel decision on the pork industry "seriously departed from a fundamental rule of procedure and manifestly exceeded its powers, authority or jurisdiction." The Committee, composed of three retired judges, met to consider the U.S. allegations. On June 14, 1991, it unanimously dismissed the allegations and reinstated the panel decision of January 1991. As a result of this decision by the Extraordinary Challenge Committee the U.S. government will return $20 million dollars in duties collected from the Canadian industry and will rescind the duty it had imposed.

Chapter 18 panels have been less successful than chapter 19 ones. The FTA foresees a procedure whereby the two governments will try to negotiate a solution to a dispute, and if that fails, then will refer the dispute to a chapter 18 panel. The agreement of the two governments is required before a chapter

18 panel can be constituted and again at several stages of a panel's work. As a result, the two governments have preferred to negotiate rather than refer issues to panels. Two issues which the Canadian government would have liked to refer to Chapter 18 panels, that of the sale of wool garments and of plywood to the United States, have not been dealt with because of objections by American authorities.

During the first two and a half years, there were only two chapter 18 panels. One panel, constituted at the request of the American government, dealt with a Canadian regulation which required that all salmon and herring caught off the West Coast of Canada be landed in Canada to be counted, ostensibly for conservation purposes, but probably to ensure that processing would be done in Canada. The panel found that requiring one hundred per cent of all catches to be landed in Canada was not a valid conservation measure. The two governments have since reached an agreement whereby up to 25 per cent of West Coast fish caught in Canadian waters can be landed in the United States.

The second chapter 18 panel was constituted at the request of the Canadian government and dealt with a change in a U.S. law that increased the minimum size of a lobster which can be sold in the United States. It is slightly larger (about three millimeters in fact) than that of a lobster which can be sold in Canada. The New England authorities defended their size restriction as a conservation measure. The majority of the panel ruled that the restriction on size was an internal measure, that is to say, the Canadians lost their case and eventually accepted the recommendation.

Chapter 18 panels have encountered the problems faced by many other international institutions. Given a choice, governments will usually choose not to lose control of an issue by allowing an international body to settle it. Governments would rather deal with the inconvenience of an unresolved issue than take the chance of losing.

The small Secretariat works as intended. The Canadian section has nine, the American five staff members. Bureaucratic jealousy from other parts of the two national governments has limited it to doing strictly what it was intended to do, that is service chapter 18 and 19 panels.

The Commission, consisting of the Canadian Minister for International Trade and the U.S. Trade Representative, has established a pattern of meeting every six months. The Commission meetings, thus far, seem to have been largely for show, with the real negotiations taking place in the various committees listed in Table 5 and in the Committee on the Free Trade Agreement (COFTA), a group of senior American and Canadian civil servants which prepares for the meetings of the Commission.

MISCELLANEOUS PROVISIONS. Most of the miscellaneous provisions of the FTA appear to have been carried out. Thus Canada, within a year of the coming into force of the agreement, amended its regulation with respect to cable television to require Canadian companies to pay for U.S. programs which they pick up "out of the air" and rebroadcast to Canadians. The plywood dispute, on the other hand, has not yet been resolved. The two governments have created a Binational Committee on Plywood Standards which, in turn, has delegated the task of drafting common standards to a committee of the two national standards associations.

As for the FTA provisions for consultation and notification, the Canadian Government claims that the FTA provisions have not made much difference to the way either government operates. Legislation is adopted as before, and the two embassies in Ottawa and Washington keep an eye on what may affect their citizens. The exception is legislation dealing specifically with foreign trade, where Congress has been careful to exclude Canada from most new protectionist measures.

FRAMEWORK PROVISIONS. As mentioned in chapter 4, the FTA includes a number of provisions for further negotiations. It is in this area that the least progress has been made to date, although two and a half years may be a short time if we consider that officials of the two governments have concentrated their efforts on setting up the institutions and carrying out the specific provisions of the FTA.

The case of just one of the framework provisions will illustrate what is happening. During the negotiations for the FTA the two governments were unable to agree on the exact definition of what constitutes dumping or a countervailable subsidy. So they agreed that the Chapter 19 panels would be able to hear appeals from national decisions for a period of five to seven years. In the meanwhile, they would attempt to reach an agreement on the definitions.

Accordingly, the Commission during its first meeting of March 1989, established a bilateral Working Group. The negotiations began at the technical level; the Working Group held its first full meeting in November. It last met in May 1991. It decided that it would await the outcome of the Uruguay Round of the GATT negotiations, which is dealing with similar issues. Because the Uruguay Round is in serious difficulty, it may be some time before the Working Group gets to work again! No one involved in the process now believes that the two sides will be able to agree on any definitions. Two years have passed, and they have scarcely even begun the process. The most likely outcome is a continuation of the chapter 19 panel procedure.

In an interesting spinoff from these negotiations, some of the participants have suggested that it may be possible to by-pass the need for anti-dumping if the two governments agree to harmonize their competition (anti-trust) legislation. The logic behind this proposal is that domestic legislation in both countries already forbids firms' charging a low price deliberately so as to capture a market. Because charging a low price to capture a market is similar to dumping, the two governments might as well harmonize their competition legislation and provide for common standards of implementation of the harmonized legislation. Then anti-dumping rules would become unnecessary.

Even if such an agreement is reached—one senior U.S. official described the idea as visionary and impractical—it will not cover the case of subsidies and countervailing duties. If a government subsidizes an industry, thus enabling that industry to sell at lower prices, the government of a competing industry has the right to levy a countervailing duty equal to offset the subsidy received. Neither GATT nor Canadian-American negotiators have been able to agree as to what constitutes a subsidy. Both the Canadian and American governments have many programs which could be considered subsidies; for example, aid to small or minority-controlled businesses, regional development grants, or grants to promote research and development.

Almost any definition would affect existing programs on both sides of the border and would thus encounter political opposition.

While the issue of subsidies may be particularly difficult, most of the agreements to agree within the FTA have seen little progress to date. This includes the provisions on intellectual property, on services, and on government procurement. There has been progress on the more technical issues, such as the details of the definition of the rules of origin.

CONCLUSION. The formal legal provisions of the FTA have been carried out with nary an exception. The institutions have been established, and several of them are working as envisaged. However, when it comes to fleshing out the agreement with further agreements, there has been little progress to date. The short length of time that the agreement has been in force may be one reason for this. The economic recession of 1990–92 and the fact that trade negotiators' attention has been diverted by the floundering GATT talks and the negotiations for a Canada-Mexico-United States free trade agreement may be another. An even more contentious topic is that of the effects of the FTA and its relation to the Mexico talks. Those will be the subject of the next chapter.

CHAPTER 7

EFFECTS AND CONSEQUENCES

INTRODUCTORY REMARKS. Chapter 1 discussed some of the consequences which experts said might flow from freer or increased trade and contact between nations. This chapter will attempt to assess the initial impact of the Canada-United States Free Trade Agreement and make a few guesses as to its likely consequences and successors. The first section, on impact, deals with the economic impact the FTA has had on the two national economies. The second section, on successors, outlines the ongoing negotiations for a trilateral United States-Mexico-Canada free trade agreement. The third section, on consequences, deals with the initial and possible further effects the FTA has had and may have on the policies of governments in the United States and Canada.

THE IMPACT OF THE FREE TRADE AGREEMENT.
Economists, and the Canadian government, insist that it is too soon to evaluate the impact of the FTA, especially since many of the Agreement's provisions are meant to take effect only gradually. This is surprising because, as we saw in chapter 5, many of these same economists thought they could predict within a fraction of a per cent just what effect the Agreement would have on the GNP or on employment.

Some economists have nevertheless ventured estimates as to the effects of the FTA. And there may well be something to measure. The European experience has shown that a widely publicized international trade agreement has a psychological impact before any economic consequences can flow from the agreement's substantive provisions. This happened after the establishment of the European Economic Community in 1958, and again in 1988 after the announcement of the plan for a Single European Market (better known as Europe 1992).

In the case of the FTA also, businessmen and consumers started to react to the Agreement when its implementation was just beginning. As a result, the Agreement has had effects in sectors which were not even included in the FTA. Thousands of words have been written about the effects of the FTA on Canada, whereas in the United States this topic has been almost ignored. This chapter reflects this imbalance in the available information.

Effects on Canada. Much of the discussion of the effects of the FTA has consisted of a continuation of the debate about its acceptance. Those who opposed the FTA can find only negative consequences, while those who supported it find positive effects. (*See Readings Nos. 25 and 26.*) The latter especially argue that the onset of the recession of 1990–1991 has masked many of the FTA's positive effects.

Amid the confusion, it is clear that there has been no immediate increase in the degree to which Canada depends on trade with the United States. In 1988, 1989, and 1990, about 75 per cent of Canadian exports went to the United States, and 69 per cent of imports came from that source. Canada's merchandise trade surplus with the United States decreased in 1989 but increased sharply in 1990; Gordon Ritchie of the consulting firm Strategico, in a report on the FTA's second anniversary, points out that this positive balance may be due more to decreasing Canadian imports of finished products (because of the recession), than it is to greater exports.

Daniel Schwanen, writing for a think-tank, the C. D. Howe Institute, found that industries affected by the FTA show a slightly better export performance than those not so affected, but there are wide variations. Some, such as agricultural machinery, increased their exports, though they were not affected by the FTA. (Canada and the United States have had free trade in agricultural machinery since World War II.) Others, such as unprocessed wood, suffered a precipitous decline, in spite of lower U.S. tariffs.[1]

With respect to investment, the Royal Bank, in one of the few published studies which tries to gauge the over-all effect of the FTA on the Canadian economy (albeit from the point of view of a defender of the Agreement), found that during the recession, U.S. investment in Canada had slowed less than had investment from other sources; in 1990, Canada had a positive investment

[1] Daniel Schwanen, "Free Trade with Mexico: What Form Shall It Take?" *C. D. Howe Institute Commentary*, no. 31, July 1991, 10–11.

balance with the United States.[2] This was partly due to the fact that Canadian firms were investing less in the United States than they had in previous years, perhaps because they were reacting to American competition by investing more at home. A study by a multinational accounting firm showed that from 1988 to 1990, Canada was the only one of the major seven industrial countries to increase its ratio of domestic to foreign investment.[3]

The debate in Canada has centered on the manufacturing industries. From June 1988 to June 1991, manufacturing employment in Canada fell by 316,000, a decline of more than 14 per cent. This author compared these Statistics Canada data with similar figures for the United States. According to the U.S. *Monthly Labor Review*, manufacturing employment in the United States decreased by almost three million from mid 1988 to April 1991, a percentage drop of exactly 14 per cent. So the decline in manufacturing employment has been part of a restructuring within and between industries, a trend which was exacerbated by the recession, but which affected both countries to roughly the same extent.

Nevertheless, there are many cases of U.S. subsidiaries in Canada and some of Canadian companies which have moved some or all of their manufacturing operations to the United States. The Canadian Labour Congress and the Council of Canadians publishes lists of such occurrences every six months. The supporters of free trade counter with "success stories," incidences of firms which have increased employment in Canada or restructured by concentrating one or two product lines in Canada. Sometimes the same companies appear on both lists. Thus Campbell Soup is said both to have increased investment in Canada and to have closed plants; Northern Telecom is also cited as an example by both sides in the debate, though that firm has clearly cut employment. It is said to have expanded operations, also to have closed plants in Quebec and moved the jobs to the United States.[4]

---

[2]*Econoscope* (Royal Bank of Canada), February 1991, 4.
[3]*Globe and Mail*, April 1, 1991.
[4]Both of these stories about Northern Telecom appeared in the same issue of the *Toronto Star*, Dec. 13, 1990.

The Royal Banks' survey of major Canadian industries identified industries which have been affected by United States-Canada free trade. Those industries which critics expected to suffer most from the FTA have done so (food processing, textiles, furniture). The furniture industry, for example, has suffered both because of a higher Canadian dollar and a lower tariff. As a result, many Canadian retailers are now buying furniture from the United States.

The FTA was supposed to lead to more secure access for Canadian firms to the American market. Since January 1989, Canadian industries have not been subjected to any new restrictive measures by U.S. legislation. However, a number of restrictive measures which should have been removed because of the FTA are still in place, though one which the FTA confirmed has since been removed. This was the agreement of December 1986, by which the Canadian government agreed to tax most softwood lumber exports so as to make them less competitive in the United States. In September 1991, the Canadian government announced that it would no longer levy this tax. (See Chapter 6 for more on the implementation of the FTA.)

There are also unofficial restrictions such as the restraint Canadian steel companies practice when they export to the United States. Canadian media carry many stories of possible new restrictions on Canadian exports. One which could be significant is the March 1992 decision by the U.S. Customs Service which found Honda Canada not to be complying with the 50 per cent North American origin provisions of the Autopact. As the rules defining North American content are complex, there is some room for discretion in such an "audit."

With respect to energy, Canadian natural gas producers especially have greatly increased their sales to the United States, and this has led to pressure in Congress to restrict Canadian imports. In agriculture, the effect of the world-wide depression of cereal prices has been much greater than has that of the FTA. The Canadian government has accused the American government of breaking an FTA commitment not to subsidize wheat sales to traditional Canadian exports markets. Southern Ontario fruit and vegetable producers are feeling the competition of American produce grown under more favorable climatic conditions; Canadian food processors are in many cases free to buy cheaper American products.

The main psychological impact of the agreement in Canada has been in Canadian border towns, where shopping in the United States appears to have become a way of life. From June 1988 to June 1991, day trips by Canadians into the United States increased from 3.1 to 5.2 million per month. Many of the the goods these shoppers bring back would not qualify under the FTA's rules of origin or should be subject to federal and provincial taxes, but the sheer volume of traffic has made enforcement of customs rules impossible. This may not have a major effect on the balance of trade, but it has hurt Canadian retailers.

From the point of view of the supporters of the FTA, almost everything seems to have conspired to nullify any positive effect the Agreement may have had on Canada. The rise in the value of the Canadian dollar more than cancelled out the initial reduction in tariffs, made U.S. goods cheaper in Canada, and made Canadian goods dearer in the United States. High interest rates in Canada frustrated the investment which was supposed to make Canadian industry more productive. The Canadian government did not implement the training and adjustment programs it had promised. On the East Coast, where fishermen were supposed to benefit from lower U.S. tariffs, a precipitous fall in fish stocks has caused the industry to decline. Given these unfavorable circumstances, it is truly impossible to judge the impact of the FTA on the Canadian economy. Perhaps, as Canada's International Trade Minister said on August 17, 1991, the recession would have been worse without the FTA, or perhaps, the FTA's opponents say, the effects of the recession would have been less severe without it. This is an issue the reader will have to judge.

Effects on the United States. As in the case of Canada, there has been no dramatic shift in the proportion of trade going to the other FTA partner. As a percentage of total American exports, exports to Canada declined somewhat from 1987 to 1990, as the following figures indicate:

1987	1988	1989	1990
24.8%	23.2%	22.3%	21.4%

On the import side, American imports from Canada have remained the same at about 18 per cent of total American imports.

Trade with Canada is much less important to the United States than trade with the United States is to Canada. Eighteen per cent of Canada's GDP depends directly on trade with the United States; less than two per cent of America's GDP depends on trade with Canada. It is, therefore, difficult to assess the impact of any change in trade with Canada on the U.S. economy; such an attempt might be compared to trying to trace the path of a drop of water through the ocean. Nevertheless, Jeffrey Hawkins of the U.S. Department of Commerce claimed in April 1992 that from 1990 to 1991, the FTA "may have accounted" for 28,000 job creations in the U.S. (*Business America*, April 20, 1992).

An American business magazine which investigated the effect of the FTA on U.S. business found that both the small businessmen and the middle managers interviewed showed little interest in the FTA. If they did sell to Canada, they found the tariffs insignificant, but the paperwork required to prove the American origin of goods was a deterrent to sales in Canada. One exception was a furniture company in Pulaski, Virginia, which had seen "a spurt" in sales to Canada.[5] This accords well with Canadian observations. The furniture industry is one of those which has been most affected.

The impact of the FTA on the United States can be gauged mainly in relation to specific industries or regions. As in the case of Canada, claims of damage have to be assessed carefully. In January 1990, the last of New Mexico's fifty-five uranium mines shut down amid claims that the FTA was partly responsible. But the other fifty-four mines had closed before 1989.

The FTA has had an effect on some of the states and regions bordering on Canada. New York state has probably benefitted the most; Michigan and North Dakota have also gained. Cross-border shoppers are responsible for some of this gain, but there are other factors. Many of the Canadian firms which have opened new American offices or have moved part of their operations to the United States have gone to the Buffalo area.

---

[5] Patricia Carey, "The Truth about Free Trade," *North American International Business*, April 1991, 22–26.

Here again the psychological effect of free trade seems to have been paramount. The peak year for Canadian firms moving to New York state was 1988. That year seventy-eight Canadian firms moved there; in 1989 the total was sixty-eight. Grand Forks, North Dakota, has become a regional transshipment center for U.S. firms which do business in the Canadian prairie provinces, and a Canadian bus manufacturer from Winnipeg finishes its partially manufactured buses in that city.

One U.S. industry affected by the FTA is agriculture. This knowledge is available thanks to the efforts of one U.S. Department of Agriculture economist who has made a consistent effort to track the effect of the FTA.[6] She has identified several factors. First, there has been a significant increase in the two-way agricultural trade between the two countries. Second, because of the provision requiring the comparison of the subsidies to grain farmers, there has been greater transparency in the pricing mechanisms of the Canadian Wheat Board. Third, specific U.S. sectors have benefitted. U.S. meat sales to Ontario and Quebec have increased (as have Western Canadian meat sales to the American West). The fact that in May 1991 Canadian wheat subsidies outpaced American subsidies means that American firms will now be allowed to sell wheat in Canada.

Ms. Goodloe finds that the greatest impact of the agricultural provisions of the FTA has been on the agricultural policies of the two governments. Thus, Canada has moved to extend its marketing board protection for the dairy sector, while the United States is attempting to protect its sugar producers.

FROM FTA TO NAFTA—THE UNITED STATES, MEXICO, AND CANADA. Europeans distinguish between the deepening and the widening of a free trade zone or economic grouping. Deepening refers to the extension of the scope of an agreement to topics not previously covered; for example, from tariffs to taxation generally. Widening refers to the geographical extension of the area covered by an economic agreement. The sheer economic magnetism of the European Community in

---

[6]Carol Goodloe has written several papers on this topic; her findings are summarized in "U.S.-Canada Trade Pact Affects Agriculture Slightly," *Farmline*, July 1991, 15–16.

creased the membership of that group from six countries in 1958 to twelve by 1986.

In the case of the FTA, the magnet consists of a single country, the United States, which still has the largest economy in the world. Like their Canadian counterparts, Mexican leaders have come to believe that their economic progress depends at least in part on guaranteed access to the American market. As this book is about the United States-Canada Free Trade Agreement, the next section will review the recent United States-Canada-Mexico free trade negotiations as they relate to that Agreement.

The idea of a United States-Mexico free trade area or a North American free trade area (NAFTA) is not new, but it gained prominence in the 1980s as many Americans lost confidence in the multilateral trading system. (*See chapter 2 above.*) As mentioned in chapter 3, President Reagan, in announcing his candidacy for the presidency in November 1979, called for a North American free trade agreement. When Congress discussed the FTA, the idea of Mexico's joining came up from time to time. When Peter Murphy was appointed as chief negotiator for the FTA in March 1986, the announcement named him negotiator for a trade agreement with Canada *and* Mexico. Peter Murphy did negotiate a framework agreement on Mexican-American trade in 1987 (in his spare time, between negotiating sessions for the FTA), but the idea of a North American free trade agreement did not become U.S. government policy at that time.

The United States was the first of the three governments to advocate a NAFTA. In so doing, it was promoting interests some of which were similar to those it had sought to achieve during the negotiations with Canada. There were geopolitical considerations, including; the desire to have guaranteed access to Mexican energy resources (oil especially); to create a regional trade bloc which would strengthen the American position in multilateral talks or give the United States something to fall back on if those talks failed; to strengthen the U.S. position in the Western hemisphere by forestalling Japanese and European involvement and investment; and to ensure that Mexico's economic liberalization would and could not be reversed. On a personal level, President Bush's special interest in Latin America paralleled Reagan's enthusiasm for free trade with Canada.

Two American political interests which were peculiar to the Mexico situation were the belief that continued economic liberalization might lead to political stability and perhaps genuine democracy in Mexico, and the hope that if trade and economic liberalization would lead to prosperity, fewer Mexicans would migrate to the United States. A report on "Unauthorized Immigration" which economist Diego Asencio prepared for President Bush, stated:

We are often in the unenviable position of having to choose between accepting goods and services from our southern neighbors . . . or of countenancing unauthorized traffic in human beings. . . We are convinced that trade is the only option that offers hope to people in the area cross a broad spectrum of economic growth.[7]

Americans also held two other hopes: that better relations with Mexico would lead to cooperation and success in stopping the smuggling of illegal drugs from Mexico into the United States, and that a reward to Mexico for its economic liberalization would induce other Latin American governments to follow similar policies.

A senior member of the United States Trade Representative's Office with whom the author discussed the NAFTA confirmed that in the case of the Mexican negotiations political factors dominated, whereas the United States pursued primarily economic interests in the case of the negotiations with Canada. Yet the United States does have an economic interest in the negotiations with Mexico: the wish to expand American markets for manufactured and agricultural goods as well as services, to protect American intellectual property rights, and to have a safe and productive outlet for U.S. investment capital. In addition, Carla Hills, the U.S. Trade Representative, has claimed that if American firms can shift some of their production to low-cost Mexican plants, they will become both more profitable and more competitive, in order to export to other parts of the world and to

[7]Cited in *The Globe and Mail*, February 12, 1991.

create jobs in the United States. (*See Reading No. 27 for a summary of the official U.S. position.*)

If the United States in seeking to negotiate a free trade arrangement with Mexico after the one with Canada was basically going back for more, what the Mexican government said it hoped to achieve from such an arrangement also sounded like what the Canadian advocates of the FTA had said in 1987 and 1988. Mexicans emphasize that access to the American market will lead to the expansion of Mexican industry, and that U.S. protectionism makes guaranteed access a necessity. They also hope to attract American investment and technology to Mexico, which will be easier if investing firms know they have access to the United States. Some Mexicans have even claimed that an agreement might give Mexicans better access to the American labor market, the opposite of what representatives of the U.S. government say when they claim that a NAFTA will reduce the pressure of northward migration. Mexico's President, like Canada's Prime Minister, has pointed out that a free trade agreement could stymie the efforts of future governments which might want to reverse his government's economic liberalization measures. This in turn might make it easier for Mexico to access international capital markets. (*See Reading No. 28 for a summary of the official Mexican position.*) There was also the example and the effect of the Canadian FTA. Mexicans wanted access to U.S. capital and the U.S. market at least as good as what they believed the Canadians have obtained. So there is a link, a spillover, from FTA to NAFTA.

Canada trades but little with Mexico, though there is a growing trade in automotive products. The Canadian government's goals in entering into the American-Mexican trade negotiations have been largely defensive and relate to the FTA. Legally and politically, any future free trade agreement the United States might enter into would affect the FTA. This would be especially important for the rules of origin. If in the future Mexican-transformed goods could enter the United States and there be transformed further, they could then enter Canada under the FTA. In the case of auto parts, an industry which now has many plants in Mexico, a Mexican-American free trade agreement led to great pressure to change the definition of eligible vehicles to include those which are sixty or more per cent North American in content, as against those which are fifty per cent American or Canadian. In addition, better Mexican access to the U.S. market might in some cases mean stiff competition for Canadian goods and services. Not to mention the fact that American firms competing against Canadian firms would have access to cheaply manufactured Mexican components to which Canadian companies would have access only under a NAFTA. And Mexican firms might buy from the United States what they might otherwise buy from Canada. There was also the psychological impact of a Mexican agreement which, combined with the lower labor costs and environmental standards, could cause many American investors to seek out Mexico rather than Canada.

There were some less defensive reasons for Canadian participation in a NAFTA. A number of Canadian firms, in telecommunications and auto parts, among others, already have investments in Mexico. These and other firms expect to do well out of the projected growth of the Mexican economy. The Canadian proponents of NAFTA use many of the same arguments that they had used to defend the FTA: cheaper goods and more money for Canadian consumers, and competition which would help to rationalize Canadian industry. Furthermore, Prime Minister Mulroney is interested in Latin America; his government brought Canada into the Organization of American States. However, the defensive reasons dominated. A government which defended the FTA as a great achievement had little choice but to try and participate in the NAFTA so as to see these advantages diluted as little as possible. (*See Reading No. 29 for a summary of the Canadian position.*)

There was a lot of speculation in the Canadian press as to whether Canada would be invited to the Mexican-American talks. The fact is that both Mexican and American leaders knew that given the existence of the FTA, Canada would need to be involved and the question was only one of deciding how soon and in what form that involvement would occur. Since the NAFTA will require some amendments to the FTA, the Canadian government had every interest in participating in the Mexico-United States negotiations from the earliest possible moment. If Canada waited until the Mexican-American agreement was pretty well complete, it would have little chance of influencing the subsequent amendments to the FTA. This idea, that of a hub (the United States) and spokes (Canada, Mexico, and possibly other Latin American countries) is one that both American and Canadian leaders have rejected. Certainly, if the United States were to be the hub by negotiating first with Mexico and then turning back to Canada, it would be in a strong position to protect its interests; the Mexicans and Canadians would have no chance to collaborate on issues where their interests differ from those of the United States; for example, Mexico and Canada are both suppliers of energy; the United States, a consumer.

As is evident from the above discussion, it was the United States which had the largest interest in a NAFTA, but because of historical factors, suggestions for such a deal had to come from Mexico. They might otherwise be seen as an attempt at American domination. Given both the Bush and Reagan administration's interest in free trade within the Western hemisphere, the American government responded enthusiastically when President Salinas suggested free trade with the United States.

It is not possible to point to one day and one event and say, this is where it began. Mexico began its economic liberalization in 1985 (under a previous president), and by 1987, the country had entered GATT and signed a number of trade agreements with the United States. The Canada-United States agreement must have had a demonstration effect and may also have been more directly involved in the sense that some Mexicans feared that because of the FTA Canada could gain an advantage by attracting American investment which might otherwise go to Mexico. By 1989 newspapers throughout North America carried discussion and speculation about a possible Mexican-American free trade agreement, and think-tanks were publishing books on the topic.

In March 1990, Prime Minister Mulroney made an official visit to Mexico and signed some bilateral economic agreements. That same month, American and Mexican border states signed a series of economic cooperation agreements. In April, the Canadian government initiated a study of the possible effects on Canada of North American free trade, and in May, Carla Hills and Canada's John Crosbie discussed the possibility of a NAFTA during the FTA Commission meeting. (*On the Commission, see chapter 4 above.*)

In May 1990, the Mexican Senate approved President Salinas's proposal to hold free trade talks with the United States, and Canadian newspapers reported that the Department of External Affairs had told the Canadian government that it should participate in any United States-Mexican talks. On June 11, 1990, President Salinas made an official visit to Washington, and there the two presidents announced that they would try to achieve a bilateral free trade agreement. They sent the Mexican trade minister to Canada to brief the Canadian minister of international trade on what they had done. In August, Salinas formally requested negotiations with the United States.

In September 1990 President Bush requested "fast track" authority to negotiate the NAFTA. At the same time, the Canadian government said that it would participate. The three ministers of international trade met in December 1990 and again in January 1991, but said nothing about the results of their meetings. On February 5, 1991, the three governments announced that negotiations would begin later that year. President Bush thought the topic important enough to make the announcement at a press conference whose main subject was the Persian Gulf War.

Bush increased the pressure on Congress to give him fast track authority for these talks, and on May 23 and 24, 1991, the two houses of Congress gave Bush the authority he sought. Congress granted the administration two years to (1) negotiate a free trade agreement with Mexico *and* Canada, and (2) try to arrive at a multilateral trade agreement under GATT.

Long before that vote, officials of all three governments had been preparing for the trilateral negotiations. By March 1991, nine working groups had been set up; by June the number had increased to nineteen, and by August there were twenty. On June 12, the three international trade Ministers, Carla Hills of the United States, Michael Wilson of Canada (he had replaced John Crosbie), and Jaime Serra Puche of Mexico held their first formal session in Toronto. Working group meetings continued in all three capitals. On August 19, the ministers assembled in Seattle for the second formal session. Ministers and civil servants have revealed few details of the negotiations. Speculation in the Canadian press focused mainly on the degree to which cultural industries would be included, though there was also some discussion about arrangements for the auto industry.

The intention of these negotiations is not to revise or adapt the American-Canadian agreement, but to negotiate a new Mexican-American agreement which would provide for any necessary amendments to the FTA; that is why the agreement will be trilateral. The FTA will play a role not only because it is a legal document already binding on the United States, but because as human knowledge grows by accretion, so the NAFTA will draw on the example of the FTA. Mexicans, for example, may want to adapt the dispute settlement procedure for use in the trilateral agreement; Americans may want to use the example of the investment and energy chapters of the FTA to negotiate similar arrangements with Mexico.

Nevertheless, both Canadian and American negotiators have a secondary agenda which involves using the NAFTA talks to revise parts of the FTA. Thus, Canadians would like greater access to U.S. financial markets and to American government contracts, whereas Americans would like to increase the North American content requirements for automobiles and to include cultural industries in the NAFTA. Canadians are alert to the possibility that in some fields, such as investment or energy, Mexico may agree to less restrictive rules than Canada did. That would put pressure on the Canadian government to reopen those issues.

As of August 1991, the negotiations appeared to be going well, and officials spoke of having a draft agreement as early as February 1992. Negotiations, however, proved difficult; it was August 12, 1992, days before the Republican national convention, when negotiators for the three governments announced that they had initialled the text of a *draft* agreement. This draft contains the political compromises on which the NAFTA will be based, but lawyers and negotiators continued to work on the exact wording of an agreement. If such an agreement is completed before the November 1992 American elections, President Bush will send it to Congress for ratification. There is, however, no chance that Congress will complete its deliberations before the elections. The fate of NAFTA will, therefore, depend on the next U.S. President and the next U.S. Congress. Canada must also hold a national election by 1993, and Mexico will elect a new president.

BEYOND NORTH AMERICA. President Bush is a fervent advocate of a wider free trade area, encompassing all or most of the countries of the Western hemisphere. At his February 5,

1991, press conference, where he announced the trilateral trade negotiations, he spoke of "a dramatic first step towards the realization of a hemispheric free trade zone, stretching from . . . Alaska to the Straits of Magellan." Some Latin American leaders have spoken in support of similar ideas. The Mexican government has said it is negotiating further trade deals with other Latin American nations. Caribbean leaders are concerned that any advantage that they derived from the limited unilateral U.S. trade concessions of the 1986 Caribbean Basin Initiative will be diluted by the NAFTA. And authorities in some of the other Latin American countries fear that Mexican producers will gain an advantage in the American market. For all these reasons, it seems likely that NAFTA may expand to include other Western hemisphere nations.

The creation of a Western hemisphere free trade zone officially became U.S. policy on June 17, 1990, when President Bush announced his "Enterprise for the Americas" (which also included plans for debt relief). It is not possible to say whether and when such a free trade zone will be created. Since the Mexican agreement will need to be completed first, much will depend on the next presidential elections in the United States and Mexico and on events in Latin America. American representatives, daunted by the complexity of further negotiations with each Latin American country, have suggested that the Latin Americans form trade groupings among themselves before beginning talks with the United States. Yet the August 12, 1992 NAFTA includes a provision for the accession of other countries.

Was there a grand plan, one which led from FTA to NAFTA to Enterprise for the Americas? Probably not. A number of prominent Americans, including Presidents Reagan and Bush, favor a Western hemisphere trade bloc, and they have been able to work their way toward the fulfillment of this idea as the opportunities presented themselves. Canadians were engaging in a nation-wide debate about free trade before they had any encouragement from an American government. And Mexican governments began to liberalize and deregulate that country's economy before they began to talk to Americans about freer trade. Any further extension of the NAFTA will depend on similar initiatives from other Western hemisphere governments.

That is not to say that there is no direct connection between the creation of the original FTA and its progenitors. As the grouping becomes larger it becomes more attractive to out-siders. And to the extent that it is seen to foreclose or reduce the markets, the capital, or the political support nations outside NAFTA can enjoy, the free trade zone induces other nations to join. This is clear from our earlier discussion of the process that led from FTA to NAFTA; barring a major change in political direction in the United States, it will no doubt continue to be true. So there is a process of widening, of extension, which has caused the FTA to spread outward.

THE DEEPENING OF THE FTA. Chapter 1 discussed some of the consequences which statesmen, such as Cordell Hull, and political theorists, such as David Mitrany, expected to follow from freer trade and more frequent contact among peo-ples in different nation-states. Chapter 5 recounted how Cana-dians who opposed the FTA expected it to cause Canada to become more like the United States and perhaps even to become a part of that country. The following paragraphs will make a cursory attempt to assess the extent to which these processes have occurred.

The first question to consider is whether the degree of eco-nomic integration provided for in the FTA has begun to lead to further economic integration. The answer is yes. To date this is most notable in the field of tariffs. The FTA has led to pressure to harmonize Canadian and American tariffs as against the rest of the world. In the case of auto parts and textiles, for example, the Canadian tariff is higher than the American one. Canadian manufacturers of automobiles and clothing want these tariffs reduced because American manufacturers can buy supplies from Mexico or India more cheaply than can their Canadian counterparts. Another example is that of the harmonization of technical standards. As mentioned in chapter 6, the two govern-ments have not yet made arrangements for such mutual recogni-tion. In the meanwhile, firms in various fields have got together to draft common standards. The manufacturers of heating and ventilating equipment did so in 1990, and the manufacturers of electrical equipment may be the next. In a related field, the U.S. government has designated the metric system as the preferred system of measurement in international trade. (Canada has been using the metric system for the past fifteen years, as do most other industrialized countries.) The American government has also begun to revise the laws governing banking in the United States. However, the fact that Canada's large federally regulated banks can operate in the United States more freely than they did before the FTA is only one factor in this proposed revision, which is overdue because of world-wide competitive pressures on American banks.

Some other legislation may be harmonized because of the FTA; for example, the regulation which requires Canadian universities to declare that no suitable Canadians are available before they can hire an academic from outside the country, or laws providing for compulsory drug testing of long distance truck drivers. Air transportation is another area that may be integrated. On October 3, 1990, the U.S. Transportation Secretary and his Canadian counterpart announced that they would begin negotiations for "Open Airline Markets" because the FTA "had created a new economic environment that makes more flexible travel necessary.[8] As in the case of technical standards, the private sector has anticipated such an agreement; in April 1992, American Airlines and Canadian Airlines began a number of cooperative ventures.

The next question to consider is whether free trade has caused the political systems of the two countries to become more like each other. This has happened but to a very limited extent. In order for the dispute settlement mechanisms to function Canada had to set up a procedure for dealing with complaints about subsidized and dumped imports which resembled that of the United States. This was, in fact, done before the FTA came into force. Canada has altered some of the procedures used to review bids for government contracts in order to comply with the government procurement provisions of the FTA. These two administrative changes, however, do not compare with the influence that the American political system exerts on the Canadian through the U.S. media, an influence which is independent of the FTA and predates it by many years. Increasing person-to-person contact, such as that between business leaders, or that of cross border shoppers, may lead to further changes in political attitudes and hence institutions.

[8]*Washington Post*, October 4, 1990.

It is difficult to assess whether the FTA has made any difference in Canadian foreign policy because the government that has been in office in Ottawa since 1988 is in any case inclined to follow a policy similar to that of the Republican administration in Washington. On January 12, 1991, the *Globe and Mail*, a paper which is generally favorable to the Conservative government, reported that Canada's faithful stand during the Gulf War would be rewarded with participation in the Mexican trade negotiations. President Bush did announce this participation on February 5, but as pointed out above, Canada would in any case need to be involved in NAFTA. Perhaps its Gulf War stand helped Canada to achieve an earlier involvement. On February 20, the same newspaper reported that Congressman Wyden from Oregon feared that because of Canada's support during the Gulf War the lumber industry in his state would not get sufficient protection against Canadian imports. So it is possible, but by no means proven, that the FTA has had some effect on Canadian foreign policy.

The last question to consider is whether the FTA has led to policy integration, that is to common policy-making, by the two governments. Once again it is difficult to judge because the two governments have long consulted extensively on a number of issues, such as safety and environmental standards for automobiles or GATT negotiations. One field where the FTA does appear to have contributed to common policy making is that of visa and immigration policy. The Canada-United States Commission has revised the list of professions which can cross the border for temporary entry several times and has added definitions for qualifications of various professions. There is also increasing evidence that the American government is interpreting "temporary entry" so liberally that some Canadian professionals are able to use it as a means of immigration to the United States.

So overall there has been a limited degree of integration due to the FTA, but because the Agreement has been in effect for such a short period of time, it is not possible to say just how much more integration will result from it.

IN PLACE OF A CONCLUSION

The remarks which follow evaluate the FTA from three points of view: Is it free trade? Does or could it contribute to international peace and understanding? Has or could it contribute to the welfare of the individual human being?

In a historical context, the Canada-United States Free Trade Agreement is one of hundreds of such trade agreements governments have concluded over the last two hundred years. Governments have entered into trade liberalization agreements for a variety of economic and political motives. In most cases, a combination of the economic motives, that is the search for wealth, and the political motives, that is the search for power to impose one's will or one's vision, worked together to produce an agreement for freer trade. The European Community, for example, arose from a complex mixture of political and economic factors, as have most Canadian-American free trade agreements. The history of freer trade is no place to look for the predominance of economic motivations, much less to demonstrate economic determinism.

The FTA-NAFTA fits into this pattern. The discussion in chapters 3, 5 and 7 demonstrates the extent to which the three governments involved have sought not only greater wealth but the ability to impose their vision of economic organization, that of government supervised free enterprise, when they concluded the FTA and began to negotiate the NAFTA.

As mentioned above, most free trade agreements are in fact agreements for somewhat freer trade. Paradoxically, *freer* trade may amount to less freeing of trade than would total free trade. Judged by this standard, the FTA, does not fare particularly well. It excludes many goods and most services. In terms of the amount of trade covered, the FTA looks somewhat more significant. Canada and the United states do more two way trade than any other two countries in the world; an agreement liberalizing that amount of trade makes a major contribution to the liberalization of world trade.

Chapter 1 described some of the benefits that its fervent advocates have expected to flow from free trade: prosperity, which in turn would lead to harmony and peace. Chapter 7 told how the FTA has not brought prosperity to either Canada or the United States, but that could be bad luck. The two economies have continued to experience a major restructuring, from manufacturing to services, and the business cycle was approaching its nadir when the Agreement was implemented. For the next several paragraphs or so, let us give the defenders of the FTA the benefit of the doubt and assume that without it the North American recession would have been worse. That is, we shall assume that the FTA has had a positive effect on the American and Canadian economies.

Even if that were so, it would be too soon to notice any change in attitudes on the part of the people. And besides, Canadians and Americans, though there have been spats and differences, have got along pretty well over the past century. So the FTA is not likely to make much difference there. As for peace, Canada and the United States, in Karl Deutsch's felicitous phrase, form a security community, that is they would not dream of going to war against each other. Or as a wag once put it, the world's longest undefended border has become the longest undefended platitude.

The diagram in chapter 1 also pointed to another benefit theorists expected from free trade. Trade would cause contact among peoples, and people would become both more alike in their thinking and come to like each other better. A number of scholars, such as Seymour Martin Lipset, have carefully documented the differences between the American and the Canadian political cultures. In Canada, the opponents of the FTA feared that increasing economic integration would lead to political homogenization. There is now more contact between Canadians and Americans than there ever was before. More Canadians cross the border to work and shop than they did before 1988. There is less of a northward flow, but that may be partly due to the fact that the recession has reduced tourism. Will this increasing contact make the two countries and the two peoples more alike? It is, once again, too soon to tell. Changes in political attitudes, such as the Canadian deference to authority, or the acceptance of the state as a distributive agent, usually require at least a generation to take hold. So it may take another twenty years or more to determine if after the FTA Canadians began to adopt the individualistic mores of their southern neighbor.

There is yet one more way in which to evaluate the FTA. That is to judge it by the standard mentioned in the Introduction, that of the well-being of the individual human person. If the Reagan years in the United States have proved one fact, it surely must be that there is very little "trickle down" in an economy. The society at large, as represented by its various governments, must ensure that the wealth created by even the most successful economies is put within reach of its less fortunate members, be it through education, training, or social assistance. It follows that the same governments which allow business to make money by freeing trade need to ensure that large numbers of people are not left out of the national economy to become an "underclass." So far the FTA has not been able to meet the test of increasing the welfare of the individual North American. The individual American and the individual Canadian is worse off in 1991 than he or she was in 1988. That brings us back to the question raised several paragraphs ago, has the FTA made the recession worse or has it attenuated that recession? We may have to wait to see it in force in better times before we can answer that question.

If the FTA and its progenitors are to contribute to the welfare of peoples outside North America, they must, to begin with, free trade and not restrict it. The economic argument for free and freer trade is incontrovertible. Freer trade leads to a better allocation of resources. But universal free trade is probably unattainable. The modern world economy depends on a complicated framework of many types of governmental and intergovernmental laws and regulations. Thus any movement toward freer trade is likely to be partial in both the subjects and the geographical area covered. The GATT system, though its membership is increasing, is far from universal, and of the existing members many are second-class members, who either do not accept all of the system's rules and/or are not allowed all of its benefits. Multilateral freer trade does not mean world-wide free trade, although that is supposed to be its goal.

The participants in every new regional "free trade" agreement defend it as a contribution to freer world trade. Economists have no way of telling whether an agreement diverts or creates trade until a fair amount of trade diversion has taken place, and by that time the harm of restricting trade has usually been done. *The Economist* (on April 20, 1991) suggested that a simple test would be to ask the members of a trade bloc if they would accept new members. If they do, they favor free trade; if they do not, they intend to restrict it. The European Community would surely fail that test. And as for the FTA, it is a bilateral instrument designed to deal with specific bilateral problems. It would not make much sense for Japan or South Korea to ask to join. In other words, *The Economist's* test may not be practical.

Does a regional system such as the FTA, soon to become NAFTA, detract from or enhance the aim of world-wide free trade? Will the world trading system soon consist of a Fortress Europe, led by the European Community, a Fortress America, led by the United States, and perhaps a Fortress Pacific, led by Japan? If the current agricultural export war between the European Community and the United States is a sign of times to come, there could be a number of bitter trade wars: between Fortress Pacific and Fortress America in automobiles and computers, between Fortress Europe and Fortress Pacific in steel and textiles, to mention just a few possibilities. Another, less pessimistic scenario, is that these trading blocs will be subject to GATT rules, so that the multilateral system will continue to operate but will consist of a number of blocs. Such a system could be less unwieldy than the present international trading negotiations which consist of a complex series of bilateral and multilateral deals. Which one of these two scenarios is more likely? As an optimist, this writer would favor the second one, that of internationally regulated trade blocs. That is how the United Nations operates. As competition among nations turns increasingly to economic as against military means, economic blocs are likely to replace military blocs.

If the economic argument for freer trade is incontrovertible, the case for the political benefits of increasing contacts among peoples is also strong. People do not always get along better when they have more contact and get to know each other more, but they do so often enough to make the effort worthwhile. Given sufficient safeguards to protect the economically weaker members of society, free and freer trade can benefit the future of humankind. To the extent that the FTA and NAFTA do constitute this kind of free trade, they could help us all to achieve a better future.

PART II

READINGS

READING NO. 1

CORDELL HULL ON FREE TRADE[1]

In the conclusion to his memoirs, Cordell Hull gives a particularly clear statement of his perhaps somewhat naive belief in the benefits of international trade.

γ γ γ

Economic warfare results in a lowering of living standards throughout the world. It foments internal strife. It offers constant temptation to use force, or threat of force, to obtain what could have been got through normal processes of trade.

A people driven to desperation by unemployment, want, and misery is a constant threat of disorder and chaos, both internal and external. It falls an easy prey to dictators and desperadoes.

In so far as we make it easier for ourselves and every one else to live, we diminish the pressure on any country to seek economic betterment through war.

The basic approach to the problem of peace is the ordering of the world's economic life so that the masses of the people can work and live in reasonable comfort.

Nations cannot produce on a level to sustain their people in well-being unless they have reasonable opportunities to trade with one another.

And this cannot happen in a world of extreme economic barriers, political hostility, and recurring wars.

The principles underlying the trade agreements program are therefore an indispensable cornerstone for the edifice of peace.

When I was a boy on the farm in Tennessee, we had two neighbors—I'll call them Jenkins and Jones—who were enemies of each other. For many years there had been bad feeling between them—I don't know why—and when they met on the

[1]*The Memoirs of Cordell Hull*. London: Hodder & Stoughton, 1948, vol. I, 364–365.

road or in town or at church, they stared at each other coldly and didn't speak.

Then one of Jenkins's mules went lame in the spring just when Jenkins needed him most for plowing. At the same time Jones ran short of corn for his hogs. Now it so happened that Jones was through with his own plowing and had a mule to spare, and Jenkins had a bin filled with corn. A friendly third party brought the two men together, and Jones let Jenkins use his mule in exchange for corn for the hogs.

As a result, it wasn't long before the two old enemies were the best of friends. A common-sense trade and ordinary neighborliness had made them aware of their economic need of each other and brought them peace.

Yes, war did come, despite the trade agreements. But it is a fact that war did not break out between the United States and any country with which we had been able to negotiate a trade agreement. It is also a fact that, with very few exceptions, the countries with which we signed trade agreements joined together in resisting the Axis. The political line-up followed the economic line-up.

READING NO. 2

THE ECONOMIC ARGUMENT FOR FREE TRADE[2]

In a supplement to its September 22, 1990 issue, the British weekly news magazine The Economist *makes a strong case for freer international trade. The original article, which is about twenty pages long, includes many diagrams and examples intended to convince those who have little formal training in economics. The following excerpts cite only the general principles to which the examples relate.*

γ   γ   γ

In a series of trade rounds, governments cut the average tariff on manufactured goods from 40% in 1947 to less than 10% by the mid-1970s. Since then the average tariff has fallen even further, to roughly 5%. In addition, by the late 1950s, the industrial-country governments had a modern system of international exchange and payments, with fully convertible currencies. As a result, tariff liberalisation spurred remarkably rapid growth in world trade. Between 1950 and 1975 the volume of trade expanded by as much as 500%, against an increase in global output of 220%.

The instruments of this spectacular change in the character of the world economy were the three guiding principles embodied in the articles of the GATT:

• **Reciprocity.** If one country lowers its tariffs against another's exports, it can expect the other country to lower its tariffs in return. . . .

• **Non-discrimination.** This principle says that countries should not grant one member or group of members preferential

[2]*The Economist.* September 22, 1990, S7, S8, S15, S16, S38 and S40.

trade treatment over the others. It is known as the most-favoured-nation (MFN) rule. . . .
• **Transparency.** The GATT urges countries to replace non-tariff barriers (import quotas, for instance) with tariffs, and then to 'bind' those tariffs (that is, promise not to raise them again). . . .

In this way, the benefits of bargains struck by the governments of big economies with lots of clout . . . are automatically extended to smaller countries, which might otherwise be left out. At the same time, the system makes sure that any initial spark of liberal intentions is fanned into a healthy flame. That was the theory and in the areas of world trade to which it was applied, that was how it worked.

The world's extraordinary economic progress since the second world war owes a great deal to the flame of international trade. . . .

Trade does not equalise incomes when productivity differs across countries, [sic] it just makes all sides better off than they would otherwise be. Moreover, trade always uncovers opportunities of this kind. . . .

A tariff will increase a country's production of the protected good and raise the price paid to producers. . . . The government collects some extra revenues too. But consumers buy less of the good than before and have to pay more for it, so they lose. Consumers lose more than the combined gain of producers and the government. Therefore stick with free trade. . . .

Protection takes the competitive pressure off producers, and therefore fosters inefficiency. . . . Also, if practiced on a large scale . . . protection denies the economy access to new techniques: imports often supply both the spur and the means to innovate. . . .

In the beginning, the GATT was a smallish group of fairly like-minded countries. Accordingly, the idea of a co-operative march to more liberal trade was plausible. As the membership grew, co-operation became more difficult. A north-south division emerged. . . .

America has substantially raised its protectionist barriers—and barriers of the most damaging kind—during the past decade. In Europe, Project 1992 seems certain to promote freer trade within the E[uropean] C[ommunity], but a willingness to promote freer trade with outsiders is still in question. . . .

If governments genuinely want freer trade, they would use the existing GATT to bring it about. Moreover, in that case, regional free-trade deals need pose no threat to liberalisation across a broader front. . . .

The GATT has always been a good tool—but only a tool. Now that the developing countries are at last starting to come around to free trade, it can work better than ever before.

READING NO. 3

THE HISTORICAL ARGUMENT FOR FREE TRADE[3]

This extract from the annual economic report President Reagan's advisors sent to Congress in February 1985 makes the best possible historical case for free trade.

γ　　　　　γ　　　　　γ

The persuasive power of arguments for free trade arises not from abstract economic reasoning, but from concrete historical comparisons of the achievements of free trade against those of protectionism. The conclusions to be drawn from such comparisons over the past two centuries are unambiguous: Countries that have followed the least restrictive economic policies both at home and abroad have experienced the most rapid economic growth and have enabled the greatest proportion of their populations to rise above subsistence living standards. . . .

The Achievements of Free Trade

The power of free trade is amply demonstrated in history, including the early history of the United States. Under the Articles of Confederation, protectionist interests in individual States moved quickly to restrict the flow of competing products from other States. The debilitating effects of this protectionism on the States' economies convinced the framers of the U.S. Constitution to forbid individual States from levying tariffs (and the Federal Government from levying export duties). Federal courts have guarded the integrity of this prohibition, ruling as recently as 1981, for example, that a Louisiana tax on natural gas passing through the State was unconstitutional. The constitutional ban on State tariffs was crucial to the development of the

[3]*Economic Report of the President*. Transmitted to Congress, February 1985. Washington: United States Government Printing Office, 1985, 115–116.

U.S. economy not only because it established a free-trade area among the 13 original States, but also because it ensured that the free-trade area would expand automatically as new States joined the Union.

A second experience that illustrates the power of open markets is Britain's movement toward freer trade in the middle of the 19th century. There are two salient features of this experience. First, Britain's move was unilateral. The repeal of the Corn Laws by Robert Peel's government in 1846 was not conditional upon "concessions" from Britain's trading partners. Rather, the repeal was motivated by the growing recognition that the tariffs on imported grain set by the Corn Laws were a barrier to the advancement of Britain's own economy. Second, the results of free trade were exactly opposite to predictions that a decline in the prices of imported grains from repeal of the Corn Laws would lead to a corresponding decline in wages. Rather than falling, however, wages rose rapidly due to growth. Thus, Britain was very much an "engine of growth" in the 19th century world economy, and freer trade fueled the engine.

More recent experiences sustain the point. The slide of the world economy into the Great Depression of the 1930s was accelerated by unprecedented tariffs imposed by the Smoot-Hawley Act of 1930 and by similar measures abroad. In response to such disastrous protectionism, the U.S. Secretary of State, Cordell Hull, organized passage of the Trade Agreements Act of 1934, which became the basis for multilateral trade liberalization. Further trade liberalization, however, was delayed until after World War II. Significantly, 1984 marked the 50th anniversary of the Trade Agreements Act.

Since World War II, successive rounds of multilateral trade liberalization have demonstrated the power of open markets through almost four decades of world economic growth. After full implementation of the current Tokyo Round tariff cuts in 1987, import tariffs among major industrialized countries will average below 5 percent on industrial products, down from averages of more than 50 percent at their peak in the 1930s. These cuts have played a central role in the post-World War II expansion of the world economy.

During the same period, the emergence and expansion of the European Community liberalized trade even further among

Western European countries. As the United States had done almost two centuries earlier, the members of the EC accelerated their economic growth by establishing a large, relatively unrestricted common market. The opening of the European market has been central to Western Europe's economic growth.

A final illustration of the achievements of freer trade is particularly important. As former colonies gained independence after World War II, they typically sought to achieve economic independence as well. Many embarked upon extensive import substitution policies to reduce their dependence on imports from former colonial trading partners. The overwhelming conclusion of studies of these policies, however, is that they severely stunted economic growth. In contrast, those developing countries that pursued more open economic policies have experienced truly remarkable records of economic growth. Recent examples include Hong Kong, Singapore, Taiwan, and South Korea, among others.

READING NO. 4

THE ARGUMENT AGAINST FREE TRADE[4]

Arghiri Emmanuel, a professor of economics at the University of Paris VII, gives lengthy economic proofs for his argument that free trade may not always be beneficial. The following arguments are drawn from his conclusions.

γ γ γ

What worsens is not the terms of trade of certain *products* but those of certain *countries*. . . . We have had to look at equivalence inside the nation . . . under conditions of mobility (or rather of competition) of the factors, and then outside the nation, that is under conditions of immobility (or noncompetition) of one or more factors. . . .

Finally, after we had studied the relative disadvantages that the low-wage countries may suffer from free trade, it remained to refute . . . that a general advantage accrues . . . to the world as a whole from free trade and the international division of labor, but showing that under conditions of regional disparity is rewarding of the factors . . . nothing guarantees that specialization . . . shall . . . result in the sought-for world optimum. . . .

What must the underdeveloped countries now do in face of the . . . continued worsening of their terms of trade? . . . They can only seek means to keep for themselves . . . the excess surplus value that they extract from their own workers. . . .

It was through tariffs and direct legislative coercion that England made India her supplier of cotton and Australia her storehouse of wool—something . . . that had the effect of ruining India but enriching Australia . . . when we consider all this, we . . . harbor a few doubts as to the intrinsic value of the international division of labor.

[4]*Unequal Exchange* (New York: Monthly Review Press, 1972), 266–270.

. . . If . . . a vehicle-hour is worth four or five times as much on the world market as a cotton-textile hour . . . [a country] may well find that her advantage lies in producing her own vehicles rather than acquiring them in exchange for her cotton goods, despite the considerable difference in productivity. If world economy does not find this to *its* advantage . . . this is not something [the country] has to worry about.

. . . If the very concept of a world economy has any meaning . . . it will . . . be necessary . . . to set up internationally at least such mechanisms of redistribution as already exist on the national scale.

READING NO. 5

JOHN A. MACDONALD'S
NATIONAL POLICY[5]

John A Macdonald introduced the following motion in the Canadian House of Commons on March 13, 1878. When Macdonald returned to office as Prime Minister later that year, the motion became government policy, and has since been known as the "National Policy."

γ   γ   γ

. . . it be *resolved*, that this House is of opinion that the welfare of *Canada* requires the adoption of a National Policy, which, by a judicious readjustment of the Tariff, will benefit and foster the Agricultural, the Mining, the Manufacturing and other interests of the Dominion; that such a Policy will retain in *Canada* thousands of our fellow countrymen, now obliged to expatriate themselves in search of employment denied them at home, will restore prosperity to our struggling industries, now so sadly depressed, will prevent *Canada* from being made a sacrifice market, will encourage and develope [sic] an active interprovincial trade, and moving (as it ought to do) in the direction of a reciprocity of Tariffs with our neighbours, so far as the varied interests of *Canada* may demand, will greatly tend to procure for this Country, eventually, a reciprocity of Trade. . . .

[5]*Journals of the House of Commons of the Dominion of Canada*, From the 7th February 1878 to the 10th May 1878 Being the 5th Session of the 3rd Parliament of Canada, [Ottawa]: House of Commons, [1878], vol. XII, 78.

READING NO. 6

HOW RECIPROCITY 1854 CAME TO AN END[6]

In his case study of Portland, Maine, the Canadian historian Dr. Graeme Mount shows how a mixture of economic and nationalistic factors convinced Maine's representatives in Washington to support the cancellation of the 1854 Reciprocity Treaty.

γ   γ   γ

Continental economic integration—stronger trade links between Canada and the northeastern United States—promised new returns on Portland's traditional commercial advantages.

The key to linking Canadian trade to Portland's port facilities was the Atlantic and St. Lawrence Railroad . . . which joined Montreal and Portland. . . .

Given the importance of the Canadian connection . . . , one might . . . look for strong political support in Maine for diplomatic ties binding the two nations more securely. Such support, however, was not to be found. In fact, key politicians from Maine were vocal in their opposition to the Reciprocity Treaty. . . .

What exactly did Reciprocity offer to Maine's economy? . . . Maine needed coal, which could be supplied from Nova Scotia more economically than from Pennsylvania. . . . Local industries also needed specialty lumber, flaxseed, building stone and fine wool that could be shipped from British North America. Maine was far from American sources of these commodities. . . .

Reciprocity also permitted Maine's fishermen greater access to the fishing grounds off British North America. . . .

[6]Graeme S. Mount, "Maine and the End of Reciprocity in 1866," *Maine Historical Quarterly*, 26:1 (Summer 1986), 22–36.

Why, then, did so many of Maine's officeholders oppose reciprocity, despite the economic benefits it offered?. . .

Maine's fishermen, then as now, did not want to compete with fishermen from Nova Scotia, New Brunswick and Newfoundland in the United States market. . . .The Penobscot and Kennebec lumber industry suffered a setback during . . . reciprocity . . . and . . . right or wrong, lumbermen in Bangor and Augusta saw a causal connection. . . .

Shipbuilders were also opposed to reciprocity. [Representative James G.] Blaine and Frederick A. Pike, Blaine's Republican colleague . . . argued that Maine's shipbuilders needed tariff protection. . . .

Another factor that made abrogation politically acceptable was anglophobia. . . .Anglophobia was rife during and after the Civil War. Newspapers[s] . . . intimated that British business interests were behind the rapid growth of the Confederate navy. . . .

The British record during the Civil War added pressure . . . for the abrogation of reciprocity. Maine, exposed to southern raiders along its extensive coastline and to supposed British designs along its border with Canada, endorsed the national trend. . . .

Both of Maine's senators, Nathan A. Farwell and Lot M. Morrill, expressed opposition to reciprocity. Farwell cited the need to protect jobs in the match industry in Maine. . . .Morrill . . . minimized the benefits to fishermen and argued that the Portland-Montreal rail line would survive abrogation. . . .

Portlanders were complacent. . . .The possibility of a competing all-Canadian rail line probably did not loom large in Maine. Portland considered itself a key in the Canadian transportation system. . . .

Portland's decline as a port cannot be attributed to abrogation alone, but just as certainly renewed tariff wars and the push for an all-Canadian transportation system had a marked impact on Portland's trade.

READING NO. 7

A 1948 PROPOSAL FOR CANADA-UNITED STATES FREE TRADE[7]

The following summary of the proposed 1948 Canada-United States free trade agreement is taken from an American source. It is interesting primarily because it foreshadows some of the provisions of the 1987 agreement (items b, e, and f) and because it shows the influence of political considerations (item g).

γ   γ   γ

Memorandum by the Associate Chief of the Division of Commercial Policy (Willoughby) to the Assistant Secretary of State for Economic Affairs (Thorp)

TOP SECRET

[Washington, undated, but enclosed with a memorandum dated March 8, 1948]

Outline of Proposal

(a) Immediate removal of all duties by both countries.

(b) Prohibition of all quantitative restrictions on imports after 5 years except that (1) the United States would retain right to impose absolute quotas on imports of wheat and wheat flour, and (2) Canada would retain right to impose absolute quotas on imports of certain fresh fruits and vegetables during Canadian growing season.

(c) The United States would retain right to impose absolute transitional (5-year period) quotas on certain products now subject to tariff quotas (most of the sensitive items from the United States standpoint), with provision for progressive increase in quotas during 5-year period.

---

[7] *Foreign Relations of the United States, 1948*, vol. IX, *The Western Hemisphere*, Washington: Government Printing Office, 1972, 407.

(d) Canada would retain right to impose absolute transitional quotas on certain products during 5-year period, with provision for progressive increase in quotas during period.

(e) Provision would be made for joint consultation, particularly for working out joint marketing agreements for agricultural products.

(f) Any controls imposed on exports of short-supply items would be made subject to principle of equal sacrifice and equal benefit, and advance consultation would be required before imposition of such controls.

(g) Consideration is being given to a clause ensuring, in the event that one country is subject to military attack, continued free access to the products of the other.

READING NO. 8

CANADA'S SENATE SUGGESTS FREER TRADE WITH THE UNITED STATES[8]

This extract from the conclusions of a 1978 report by the Canadian Senate Standing Committee on Foreign Affairs already expresses many of the concerns about competitiveness that were to surface during the debate of the 1980s. The Senate, and therefore, the Committee had a Liberal Party majority.

γ   γ   γ

Starting from the perception that serious measures have to be taken to improve Canada's competitive capacity, the Committee has considered each of Canada's principal options.

- It rejects increased protection as leading inevitably to diminished competitiveness and a declining standard of living.
- It supports general tariff reductions under the GATT, on condition that non-tariff measures are . . . dismantled, but is sceptical regarding . . . the results. . . .
- It makes recommendations for strengthening the competitive capacity of Canadian industry, but concludes that these measures by themselves are insufficient to achieve the rationalization needed by Canadian manufacturing.
- It sees no prospect for general free trade and counsels strongly against . . . unilateral free trade. The preferred arrangement would be . . . sectoral free trade arrangements with the United States . . . but it is unlikely such an approach would be of interest to the United States. . . .

---

[8][Senate of Canada], The Standing Senate Committee on Foreign Affairs, *Canada-United States Relations*, vol. II, *Canada's Trade Relations with the United States*, Ottawa: Queen's Printer, 1978, 120–121.

. . . The Committee has concluded that, in order to resist the gradual shift of Canadian manufacturing capacity to the United States and to strengthen potentially competitive firms and industries in Canada, Canadians should seriously examine the benefits to be derived from free trade with the United States. It is not a policy without risk, but the Committee is convinced that the balance of advantage from bilateral free trade with the United States is greater than most witnesses perceived for the following reasons:

a) An exchange rate differential can provide a more general and effective protection than the tariff. . . .

b) Without unimpeded access to the United States market, it will be difficult—even with government encouragement—to rationalize industrial production and for Canada to become more competitive. As tariffs decline, the pressure from abroad, including the United States, for more effective non-tariff barriers may grow and Canada may find itself increasingly squeezed out of the US market. Only a blanket exemption for Canada, which should be negotiated as part of a free trade arrangement, could avoid this risk, and reverse the trend for US companies to close their Canadian subsidiaries and for Canadian companies to move southward.

c) . . . Average wage rates in Canada have in the last few years grown to the point where they equal or exceed those in the United States. Bilateral free trade should now be perceived as a discipline to hold Canadian wage rates in line.

d) . . . A bilateral free trade agreement with the United States should be entered into in stages over a minimum of ten years.

READING NO. 9

AN AMERICAN ARGUMENT
FOR BILATERALISM[9]

These extracts from the opening pages of Dornbusch's chapter on bilateralism constitute one of the clearest and most articulate statements of this option of U.S. foreign trade policy.

γ   γ   γ

U.S. TRADE POLICY should aggressively seek freer trade, complementing the GATT process with bilateral initiatives. The policy should aim at rolling back domestic nontariff barriers, securing the opening of markets abroad, and forestalling the emergence of trade blocs harmful to U.S. exports. How should these goals be achieved? . . . The public debate portrays trade policy as if there were only two options: the status quo of "GATT and the open, multilateral system" (which is neither quite open nor uniformly multilateral) and "managed trade" (the Gatt-is-dead crowd). . . .Anyone arguing for bilateral liberalization falls into the crossfire between protectionists who see the risks for vulnerable industries, and never see the potential for extra exports, and multilateralists who fear for the process. . . .

In the United States, commitment to the GATT process has become an objective in itself. Americans automatically object to bilateral initiatives, even ones that are plainly within the GATT rules. . . .Few among the protagonists of the status quo ask whether the protracted GATT process—negotiations take a decade or more—will deal adequately with the biggest problems facing U.S. trade policy. . . .

[9]Rudiger W. Dornbusch, "Policy Options for Freer Trade: the Case for Bilateralism," in Robert Lawrence and Charles Schultze, eds., *An American Trade Strategy for the 1990s*, Washington: The Brookings Institution, 1990, 106–108.

If there are two dirty words in international trade diplomacy, they are "aggressive" and "bilateral." The notion of aggressive policy offends in a world where negotiation, balance, and rules—diplomacy rather than bully thy neighbor—are supposed to reign. Although unilateral action, associated with Smoot-Hawley and the implosion of world trade in the 1930s, is considered the worst kind of action, bilateral action is not far behind. The liberal trading system, in this view, is fragile and might not survive the challenge of bilateral trade strategy. If the system suffers, who can be sure that it will not revert to the 1930s with pervasive impediments, collapsing trade and a world depression? Indeed, bilateralism conjures up the discriminatory trade practices of the 1930s such as Imperial Preferences and the Schacht agreements.

But the disdain for bilateralism is not warranted. Bilateralism received a bad name when it was an instrument for restricting trade, but open bilateralism or plurilateralism (a term I use interchangeably with bilateralism) can be an effective instrument for securing more open trade. Indeed, if trade is open in the sense of allowing conditional most-favored-nation access, a bilateral initiative can become a vehicle for freer trade on a multilateral basis. Third countries excluded from an initial agreement should be welcome to enjoy its benefits on condition they adhere to its terms.

. . . The policy I advocate is to use aggressive bilateralism to push the world economy towards freer trade, complementing the GATT process when it still heads in that direction or filling a vacuum in the quest for freer trade when the GATT has tacitly accepted the status quo or even a slide into protectionism. In such cases, a more forceful trade posture, exemplified by the Super 301 remedy and negotiations of free trade areas is desirable.

A bilateral approach should be oriented towards results. If other countries manage trade to restrict market access, then U.S. policy must impose performance measures in judging the success of trade policy. The United States should make continued, and preferably even less restricted, access to the U.S. market, contingent on equal treatment in targeted countries. . . .

READING NO. 10

THE MACDONALD COMMISSION RECOMMENDS FREE TRADE WITH THE U.S.[10]

The recommendation of the Macdonald Commission on Canada's Economic Prospects was the crucial factor which the Mulroney government used to justify its search for free trade with the United States. The Commission's findings were published only three weeks (September 5, 1985) before Prime Minister Mulroney made his formal request to the American government. The following excerpts give the principal reasons the commissioners used for coming to their conclusion, as well as the recommendation itself.

γ   γ   γ

. . . Canada needs to engage the United States directly and formally in the fight to resist new trade barriers, eliminate the old barriers, and generally place cross-border trade on a more secure footing. Many of our industries are competitive and prepared to grow, but they cannot do so in the face of protectionist barriers to their most important market. . . .

Existing barriers to trade, including tariffs, are real. . . . Non-tariff barriers, especially in the form of contingent protection, are most effective in denying exporters the kind of security they need. . . . On the Canadian side, our tariff remains significant and, in addition to protecting producers, raises costs to consumers and producers, and thus retards development of a more competitive economy.

---

[10]Royal Commission on the Economic Union and Development Prospects for Canada, *Report*, Ottawa: Ministry of Supply and Services, 1985, 374–5, 378–381.

Successive rounds of GATT negotiations have traditionally provided Canada and the United States with the main opportunities to liberalize cross-border trade. Future negotiations. . . , however, are unlikely to take place soon enough or to be thorough enough to provide the kind of environment Canadian producers will need by the end of the decade and beyond. We need, therefore, to engage the United States more directly in bilateral free trade negotiations.

. . . A successful agreement would include the following arrangements:

- It would establish a free trade area, rather than a customs union or common market.

- It should be a broad agreement, covering substantially all trade between the two countries, rather than a collection of sectoral agreements.

- Some sectors could be excluded from the agreement's coverage.

- It should be consistent with Canada's continued participation in GATT.

- It should apply to tariffs, contingency protection and other forms of non-tariff barriers.

- The elimination of tariffs should be phased in over a period of several years. . . .The phase-in period of the elimination of the Canadian tariff should be longer than that for the United States.

- Non-tariff barriers should be neutralized or reduced by means of common procedures and controlled by codes of conduct; these codes should provide for decision-making and implementation by a joint tribunal.

- It should provide for agreed measures of transitional adjustment assistance and safeguards.

- It should include effective dispute settlement procedures whereby national politicians jointly arrive at final decisions; compulsory arbitration by a neutral panel should be stipulated as a procedure of last resort.

- It needs to be guaranteed by national laws. . . .

Finally, our review of the political consequences of . . . free trade has convinced Commissioners that even here there are benefits. Free trade will strengthen Canada's economic fabric; it will reduce regional differences concerning the conduct of trade and industrial policy; and it will contribute to our growing sense of national confidence. Any adverse consequences can be managed by pursuing deliberate policies to strengthen cultural and other aspects of Canadian identity. Our government should also strengthen the objectives and administration of our foreign policy to reflect a more activist internationalist stance to the world community.

. . . To a great extent, Canadian trade policy has been, and will continue to be, developed as a trade-off between the business objective of securing improved access to foreign markets, the economic need to promote efficiency and competitiveness in the domestic economy, and the political need to maintain our sovereignty and freedom of action. . . .

Canada's economic growth is critically dependent on secure access to foreign markets. Our most important market is the United States. . . . More, better and more secure access to the U.S. market represents a basic requirement, while denial of that access is an ever-present threat. We are extremely vulnerable to any strengthening of U.S. protectionism. Early bilateral negotiations with the United States could provide opportunities for the two countries to negotiate reduction or elimination of tariff and other barriers to cross-border trade, at a pace and on a scale not likely to be achieved multilaterally in a further GATT round. . . .

Recommendations

■ Having carefully considered the analyses presented above, Commissioners make the following general recommendations.

■ Canadians have benefited from and contributed to the multilateral system of trade and payments . . . and we should continue to support that system as a mainstay of our foreign economic policy. . . .

■ Commissioners recommend that multilateral trade negotiations under the GATT remain a central theme of Canadian trade policy; thus Canada should move quickly to define its objectives for the forthcoming round. . . .

■ Commissioners recommend that the Government of Canada, at the same time it undertakes an initiative at the multilateral level to eliminate trade barriers, open negotiations with the Government of the United States to reach agreement on a substantial reduction of barriers, tariff and non-tariff, between Canada and the United States. Such an agreement . . . would leave each country with freedom of action to maintain separate trading policies with other economic partners. We do not recommend a more intensive arrangement such as a common market or an economic union. . . .

READING NO. 11

PRIME MINISTER MULRONEY ANNOUNCES HIS GOVERNMENT'S INTENTION TO SEEK FREE TRADE WITH THE UNITED STATES[11]

On September 26, 1985, Prime Minister Mulroney announced in the House of Commons that he had told President Reagan of his interest in pursuing bilateral free trade negotiations. Extracts from the Prime Minister's speech follow.

γ   γ   γ

Mr. Speaker . . . I have spoken today to the President of the United States to express Canada's interest in pursuing a new trade agreement between our two countries.

We hope that this action will lead to negotiations for a new trade agreement. . . . I have asked the President to explore with Congress their interest in pursuing these negotiations. Both sides recognize that the issues are complex. Both sides are determined to see the process move as expeditiously as possible.

. . . At Quebec City, six months ago, President Reagan and I . . . instructed the Minister of International Trade and the President's Trade Representative to report on how trade could be enhanced between our two countries. Today I will table the Minister's report. . . .

. . . For half a century Canada has pursued a policy of trade liberalization. Today more than ever, our prosperity and that of our partners depend on an expanding world trade and a growing

---

[11][Canada], Office of the Prime Minister, Statement by Prime Minister Brian Mulroney on Canada/US Trade Negotiations, House of Commons, Ottawa: September 26, 1985.

world economy. . . We are working to remove impediments to trade, aid, investment and development on a global basis.

In particular we are playing a leading role in promoting and preparing for a new round of multilateral trade negotiations in the GATT. . . .

No responsible person anywhere today advocates protectionism as a national economic strategy.

Yet, sector by sector, region by region, country by country, Canada included, there persists the impulse to protectionism, whenever the going gets tough. Protectionist measures are always advocated as exceptional cases.

. . . The answer to this problem lies in sound agreements, legally binding, between trading partners, to secure and remove barriers to their mutual trade . . . we must find special and direct means of securing the annual $155 billion of two way trade with the United States.

I emphasize that we are beginning a process of purely commercial negotiations with the United States, the results of which would provide sufficient time for all Canadians to plan ahead to take advantage of new opportunities from enhanced access.

We seek to negotiate the broadest possible package of mutually beneficial reductions in tariff and non-tariff barriers between our two countries.

. . . Our political sovereignty, our system of social programs, our commitment to fight regional disparities, our unique cultural identity, our special linguistic character. . . . They are not at issue in these negotiations.

READING NO. 12

THE AMERICAN GOVERNMENT DECIDES TO SEEK FREE TRADE WITH CANADA[12]

The report Prime Minister Mulroney referred to in his September 26, 1985, statement announcing the free trade initiative includes a brief report by Clayton Yeutter, then the United States Trade Representative, to President Reagan. This report recommends bilateral trade negotiations with Canada, but does so much more hesitantly than the statements by Canadian government representatives. Extracts from Yeutter's report follow.

γ　　　　　γ　　　　　γ

. . . We are committed to pursue negotiations aimed at a further liberalization of trade, be they on a bilateral, plurilateral, or multilateral basis. . . .

Earlier this year, the Canadian Government initiated a review of options for securing and enhancing trade with the United States. Canada's interest in bilateral trade liberalization with the U.S. is understandable. . . .Exports to the United States account for over 75 percent of its total exports. . . .

From preliminary, informal discussions which my staff and I have held with representatives of the private sector and Members of Congress, I believe that a number of U.S. industries have an interest in expanding their access to a prosperous and proximate Canadian market. Canada takes nearly one-fifth of our total exports, and there exist significant barriers to U.S. exports of goods and services. . . . These include:

[12]Text of Report by United States Trade Representative Clayton Yeutter to the President on Bilateral Trade with Canada, included in an untitled, unnumbered Sessional Paper submitted to the Canadian House of Commons by Prime Minister Mulroney on September 26, 1985. The report by Clayton Yeutter is dated September 17, 1985 and is found on pages 70–72 of the Sessional Paper.

- high Canadian tariffs across a wide spectrum of products. . . .
- nontariff barriers at both the federal and provincial level which effectively preclude many U.S. exports from entering the market;
- obstacles to U.S. investment; and
- federal and provincial regulations which impede U.S. exports of services.

In addition, a great many U.S. industries and Members of Congress have expressed concern over a number of governmental assistance programs, both federal and provincial, which allegedly result in subsidized competition. I have been urged to obtain in any bilateral discussions agreement on procedures to limit the use of subsidies.

My discussions with Trade Minister Kelleher indicate that the Canadian Government is prepared to seriously explore these issues. Minister Kelleher shares my belief that they could best be addressed in a bilateral negotiation which would complement your efforts to launch a new round of multilateral trade negotiations.

. . . I believe that, should bilateral trade negotiations commence, further work on government procurement, tariff barriers, barriers to trade in high technology goods and services, and intellectual property rights will be subsumed in these negotiations. Our discussions aimed at achieving an enhanced market approach in our bilateral energy trade have been successful. A good beginning has also been made in . . . facilitating travel for business and professional purposes.

READING NO. 13

THE PREAMBLE TO
THE FREE TRADE AGREEMENT[13]

The text of the preamble to and the second article of the Canada-United States Free Trade Agreement gives a reasonably accurate description of the aims and beliefs of the participants. (Please note that because of the numbering system used, Article 102 is actually the second *article of the Agreement.)*

γ   γ   γ

PREAMBLE

The Government of Canada and the Government of the United States of America, resolved:

TO STRENGTHEN the unique and enduring friendship between their two nations;

TO PROMOTE productivity, full employment, and a steady improvement of living standards in their respective countries;

TO CREATE an expanded and secure market for the goods and services produced in their territories;

TO ADOPT clear and mutually advantageous rules governing their trade;

TO ENSURE a predictable commercial environment for business planning and investment;

TO STRENGTHEN the competitiveness of the United States and Canadian firms in global markets;

TO REDUCE government-created trade distortions while preserving the Parties' flexibility to safeguard the public welfare;

---

[13]External Affairs Canada, *The Canada-U.S. Free Trade Agreement*, Ottawa: 1987, 5 and 9.

TO BUILD on their mutual rights and obligations under the *General Agreement on Tariffs and Trade* and other multilateral and bilateral instruments of cooperation; and

TO CONTRIBUTE to the harmonious development and expansion of world trade and to provide a catalyst to broader international cooperation;

HAVE AGREED as follows:. . .

Article 102: Objectives

The objectives of this Agreement . . . are to:

a) eliminate barriers to trade in goods and services between the territories of the Parties;

b) facilitate conditions of fair competition within the free-trade area;

c) liberalize significantly conditions for investment within this free-trade area;

d) establish effective procedures for the joint administration of this Agreement and the resolution of disputes;

e) lay the foundation for further bilateral and multinational cooperation to expand and enhance the benefits of this Agreement.

READING NO. 14

JAMES BAKER MAKES THE POLITICAL CASE FOR FREE TRADE WITH CANADA[14]

The extracts from this article, admittedly written in order to focus on the general benefits of the FTA, demonstrate the kind of overall foreign, and foreign economic, considerations the Reagan administration kept in mind as it negotiated and implemented the FTA. James Baker was Reagan's Secretary of the Treasury and later became President Bush's Secretary of State.

γ　　　　　　γ　　　　　　γ

According to the traditional scorecard of trade agreements—reduced tariffs and quantitative restrictions—the proposed agreement is a startling success. . . .

The sharing of natural resources, particularly in the field of energy, will be significant for our mutual security. Industrial users, homeowners, farmers, and a competitive U.S. energy sector should all gain from this, free, open, and assured trade.

Given similar challenges of adjustment in the face of heightened international competition, businesses in both nations will profit from secure access to a home-base market of about 270 million people. . . .

The proposed agreement is truly a win-win enterprise for Canada and the United States. By opening markets and establishing rules of fair play across a wide range of economic activity, we can achieve better prices for consumers and businesses and create major commercial and investment opportunities.

The agreement provides possible examples for other international arrangements as well. One of the most important is in the field of dispute settlement. . . .

---

[14]James Baker, "The Geopolitical Implications of the U.S.-Canada Trade Pact," *International Economy*, Jan.-Feb. 1988, 39–41.

[The agreement's] geopolitical potential is significant. A successful economic arrangement should enhance our ability to work together on other common problems. In the 20th century, we have maintained the longest peaceful border in the world and served with one another as allies in common defense. In the 21st century, we will also need to work closely together to better address questions concerning the environment, wildlife, ocean borders, the arctic, outer space, disease and medical science, terrorism, communications frequencies, bank and securities regulation, taxation and immigration—to name a few topics. . . .

[This agreement] is idealistic in aim, but realistic and often incremental in approach. . . .This is the spirit embodied in the Canada-U.S. Free Trade Agreement.

First, the agreement respects GATT and is careful not to undermine the successes of the multilateral approach. Canada and the U.S. are lowering barriers between themselves, not raising barriers to others. As Secretary of State George Shultz observed, we are not splintering multilateralism into bilateral agreements. Instead we are seeking a healthy, dynamic linkage between bilateral and multilateral initiatives so as to prod and reinforce the GATT.

Second, the Canada-U.S. agreement extends the reach of an open, cooperative system by negotiating solutions in the areas of services, investment and technology—while respecting national sovereignty. These arrangements demonstrate what can be achieved and offer conceptual approaches to which others may turn. . . .

Third, we have lowered the cost of initiating international liberalization in these new areas by breaking ground with only one nation at a time. . . .

Fourth, the rewards of this agreement offer an incentive to other governments. If possible, we hope this follow-up liberalization will occur in the Uruguay Round. If not, we might be willing to explore a "market liberalization club" approach, through minilateral arrangements or a series of bilateral agreements. . . .

Fifth, this agreement is also a lever to achieve more open trade. Other nations are forced to recognize that the United States will devise ways to expand trade—with or without them. If they choose not to open markets, they will not reap the benefits. By employing this lever together, the U.S. and Canada may be able to dislodge obstacles in special areas of common concern—such as agriculture.

Sixth, this Canadian-U.S. accord could prove to be an important catalyst for a domestic political coalition that wants an activist, yet constructive and internationalist, U.S. trade policy. This accord could turn out to be an attractive, bipartisan counterweight to protectionism. . . .

The Canadian-U.S. FTA could be the catalyst . . . for a new trade policy strategy. . . . The inquiries it already has elicited for similar agreements are encouraging. This interest gives the next administration . . . an opportunity to set trade policy on a creative, positive, and pragmatic international course—in a manner that is similar to Secretary Hull's a half-century ago.

READING NO. 15

PRESIDENT REAGAN RECOMMENDS THAT THE CONGRESS ADOPT THE FREE TRADE AGREEMENT[15]

In contrast to Reading No. 14, this letter which President Reagan sent to both Houses of Congress when he submitted the implementing legislation, points out most of the specific, as well as a few general, advantages the US expected to reap from the FTA. It is cleverly based on the same advantages which the committees of the House and Senate listed in their various reports.

γ   γ   γ

THE WHITE HOUSE,
Washington, July 25, 1988.

Hon. JIM WRIGHT,
Speaker of the House of Representatives,
Washington, DC.

DEAR MR. SPEAKER: Pursuant to section 102 of the Trade Act of 1974, I herewith transmit the final legal text of the United States-Canada Free-Trade Agreement, which Prime Minister Brian Mulroney and I entered into on behalf of our Governments on January 2, 1988.

With this truly historic agreement, I am submitting the proposed United States-Canada Free-Trade Agreement Implementation Act of 1988. . . .

The United States-Canada Free-Trade Agreement is one of the most comprehensive agreements on trade ever negotiated between two nations. It provides for the elimination of all tariffs,

---

[15] United States House of Representative, 100th Congress. 2nd Session, Committee on Energy and Commerce, United States-Canada Free Trade Implementation Act of 1988 [H.R. 5090], Report together with Additional Views, [Washington]: Aug. 8, 1988, 16–18.

reduces many non-tariff barriers, liberalizes investment practices, and covers trade in services. For example, the Agreement:

Significantly liberalizes Canada's foreign investment regime;

Provides secure, nondiscriminatory access to Canadian energy supplies, even in times of shortages;

Establishes the critical principle of national treatment with respect to trade in over 150 services, which will ensure nondiscriminatory treatment of U.S. services providers under future Canadian laws and regulations;

Removes essentially all existing Canadian discrimination faced by U.S. financial institutions operating in Canada;

Facilitates the temporary entry of U.S. business persons and professionals into Canada;

Freezes coverage of the United States-Canada "Auto Pact" and limits future Pact-like provisions;

Eliminates Canadian duty remission programs linked to performance requirements;

Removes the current Canadian embargo on imports of used motor vehicles and aircraft;

Expands opportunities to sell U.S. goods to the Canadian Government by extending the coverage of the GATT Government Procurement Code bilaterally to purchases between $25,000 and the Code threshold (currently about $156,000);

Provides that owners of U.S. television programs should be compensated for the retransmission of their programs in Canada;

Eliminates Canadian export subsidies on agricultural trade to the United States;

Prohibits Canadian Government and public entity sales for export to the United States of agricultural goods at prices below cost;

Generally exempts meat products of one country from the other country's meat import quota laws;

Increases Canadian poultry and egg minimum import quotas;

Sets conditions for the removal of Canadian import licensing of wheat, barley, and oats;

Establishes a forum for discussing the possible harmonization of technical regulations on agricultural trade;

Facilitates the recognition by one part of the other's testing facilities and certification bodies in the area of technical standards; and

Removes barriers to the sale of U.S.-produced wine and distilled spirits in Canada.

While I have highlighted here major benefits for the United States, the Agreement of course provides reciprocal benefits for Canada. Thus, the Agreement is a win-win situation for both countries. It will create more jobs and lower prices for consumers on both sides of the border. The overall result will be increased competitiveness and a higher standard of living in both countries.

Moreover, the Agreement looks to the future by providing a concrete example of the kind of market-opening steps the entire world should be pursuing. It thus supports U.S. efforts at trade liberalization in the Uruguay Round of multilateral trade negotiations. . . .

With this Agreement, both the United States and Canada will be better prepared to compete in the global marketplace of the 21st century. Therefore, in the interest of strengthening our economy, creating jobs, reducing consumer burdens, and advancing U.S. efforts in multilateral trade negotiations, I urge prompt approval and implementation of the United States-Canadian Free-Trade Agreement by the Congress.

Sincerely,

RONALD REAGAN.

READING NO. 16

A CONGRESSWOMAN MAKES THE CASE AGAINST THE FTA[16]

Representative Snowe, from Maine, made one of the more concise Congressional arguments against the FTA. Especially noteworthy is the fact that she accuses the supporters of the Agreement of falling for the "big picture" while ignoring the effects on specific industries.

γ　　　　　γ　　　　　γ

I certainly support the objectives of this pact to liberalize the United States-Canada trade relationship. . . .

My concern, however, is that issues of major contention for Maine and other border states have been denigrated to a lower priority level. . . .Our Trade Representative, Clayton Yeutter, testified to this effect: "It would be a terrible mistake," he said, "to evaluate this agreement on the basis of its impact on particular firms, industries, and States."

I strongly disagree with this sentiment. If we are not to evaluate the agreement's impact on industries and State economies, then what are we to look at?

. . . In the haste of our negotiators to push "the big picture," they have run rough-shod over the agricultural and natural resource industries in my State. . . .

This agreement fails to address an issue of longstanding dispute to Maine's potato, lumber and fishing industries. . . . Canada's use of Federal and provincial domestic subsidies has long hurt our workers competing in the Northeast United States marketplace.

---

[16]United States, House of Representatives, *Congressional Record. Proceedings and Debates of the 100th Congress, 2nd Session*, Washington: United States Government Printing Office, August 9, 1988, H6641–6642.

This agreement, whose primary objective is to eliminate government and industry trade barriers, completely omits steps to require the Canadians to dismantle the trade-distorting effects of domestic subsidies. . . .

Our potato industry in Maine has been fighting an uphill battle for years against an array of Federal and Provincial domestic subsidies. . . .A few years ago, Maine potato farmers watched painfully . . . as their Canadian neighbors in New Brunswick and Quebec received over $19 million to pay for dumped potatoes due to overproduction.

. . . While Canada regularly restricts the free flow of Maine potatoes into their markets with consigned sale and bulk shipment requirements, Canadian imports are annually targeted at our wide open market.

Maine fishermen have endured with difficulty against 55 Federal and Provincial subsidy programs assisting Canada's groundfish industry. The assistance provided includes vessel and shipbuilding programs and a massive Government investment to reconstruct groundfish processing facilities. Canadian fishermen, selling their fish at artificially lower prices, have captured a large foothold in our targeted American market.

State sawmill owners have watched one-fourth of their brethren disappear, right along with quantities of logs from Maine woodlands. Government-modernized sawmills located right over the border in Quebec are artificially undercutting the market.

. . . I have other concerns as well with this agreement. For example, the new bilateral dispute settlement procedure for countervailing and antidumping cases raises serious questions about protecting the sovereignty of U.S. trade statutes. When U.S. industries seek trade relief under U.S. laws, they deserve the full power of our legal rights.

. . . Finally, what about the many industries that will most definitely be hurt or destroyed by the effects of the agreement? As one example, Maine's sardine industry will lose traditional tariffs while facing a new import challenge from their government-backed competition in Canada.

. . . Mr. Chairman, I rise in opposition to this agreement. . . . The concerns of our industries, no matter how small they may appear to some, cannot be so easily cast aside.

READING NO. 17

THE AFL-CIO MAKES THE CASE AGAINST THE FTA[17]

The following extract from the AFL-CIO presentation to the Subcommittee on Trade of the House of Representatives' Committee on Ways and Means summarizes the U.S. labor movement's main objections to the FTA. Unions representing individual sectors presented some of the more specific objections.

γ   γ   γ

MR. OSWALD. Mr. Chairman and members of the committee, the AFL-CIO appreciates this opportunity to present its views on the proposed United States-Canada Free Trade Agreement. The federation believes that this agreement, signed by President Reagan and Prime Minister Mulroney on January 2, 1988, will do little to solve the serious trade problems that exist between the United States and Canada, and may in fact make them worse. The AFL-CIO joins the Canadian labor movement in opposing this agreement because we share the view that governments must play a positive role in managing relations between countries and that increased reliance on so-called market forces will not necessarily promote economic growth and equity.

Generally speaking, there is little in the agreement that will benefit American workers. It does not address the huge imbalances in trade in goods between the United States and Canada, nor the large exchange rate differential which has contributed importantly to those imbalances. Its silence on the issue of exchange rates is particularly significant, and raises real questions concerning the validity of the entire exercise.

---

[17]United States, House of Representatives, 100th Congress, 2nd Session, *Hearings before the Subcommittee on Trade of the Committee on Ways and Means*, Washington: United States Government Printing Office, 1988, Serial 100–59, pages 161–163. The date of the submission was February 26, 1988.

How can American industry and agriculture hope to compete on a fair and equitable basis when current exchange rates have the effect of conferring a 28 percent cost advantage on Canadian producers? The exchange rate advantage of the Canadians operates much like a tariff on the Canadian side of the ledger, raising the price of U.S. goods by 28 percent. But the exchange rate differential is worse than a tariff on the export of Canadian goods to the United States. It cheapens their goods by 28 percent in the U.S. market, giving them a substantial advantage over U.S. goods. . . .

The agreement is based upon the assumption that free trade between the countries will help lead the United States toward a general trade equilibrium, helping the United States in eliminating its huge trade deficits. In 1987, the United States suffered a $171 billion trade deficit, worldwide, and a $12 billion trade deficit with Canada, under one reckoning, and $18 billion under another reckoning, thus accounting for 7 or 11 percent of the U.S. trade deficit. Nothing in this agreement assures that this persistent imbalance in trade between the United States and Canada will improve.

The agreement itself, while moving in the direction of "market" determined trade, does not by any measure establish free trade. Significant inequities in trade practices remain, even after the 10-year transition period. What has been negotiated is not a free-trade agreement, but a new bilateral trade arrangement, and Congress should judge the proposal on the basis of fairness, reciprocity and national interest. Regrettably, the agreement falls far short of meeting these goals. A whole series of Canadian practices that discriminate against U.S. production have been grandfathered. By prohibiting the introduction of new measures to regulate or manage trade, Canadian advantage has been solidified.

It appears that the tradeoff for the continuation of discriminatory Canadian practices is greater access for U.S. investment and services. Even here, however, reciprocal treatment has not been achieved, and the United States has forfeited the right to employ measures that may prove necessary in the future. The AFL-CIO has long been concerned over the priority given to negotiations on investment and trade in services. The principal trade problem facing the United States is undeniably the massive trade deficits occurring in the manufacturing sector and the resultant loss of employment. Emphasis on liberalizing trade in services and investment flows will have little impact on this central issue, and may in fact contribute to the deterioration of the domestic manufacturing sector if discriminatory practices of other countries in the goods area are left intact as the price for reductions in barriers to services and investment. This problem is regrettably demonstrated by the telecommunications section of the agreement. While the United States has gained greater access for telecommunications services, Canadian procurement policies that discriminate against telecommunication goods produced in the United States remain in place. Further, what may appear to some as barriers to service trade on international investment are in fact proper and even essential social and economic policies in both the United States and foreign economies. While unrestricted flows of services and investment may be important to certain corporate interests, this does not make them significant for the economy as a whole.

The AFL-CIO is also concerned that this proposed agreement will be used as a blueprint for bilateral negotiations with other countries as well as the Uruguay round of negotiations under the General Agreement on Tariffs and Trade (GATT). Recent pronouncements by President Reagan and Vice President Bush concerning a free-trade agreement with Mexico have served to underscore that worry. The United States can ill afford to continue to ignore the damage done by one-sided trade to the domestic manufacturing sector. . . .

The separate procedures established for Canada regarding trade remedy law are not only unwise in and of themselves but establish an extremely bad precedent for negotiations with other countries. It also was concerned that the Canadian tariff advantage would continue for 10 years.

Another element was that additional Federal Government procurement would be open to Canadian bidding whereas most Canadian business or governmental activities are provincial rather than Federal.

The agreement would also permit continued Canadian protection of a variety of industries. . . .

The agreement also would weaken, in our view, U.S. emigration. It would retain favorable treatment for Canada. I [sic] would permit Canadian advantage for certain agricultural commodities and it would provide a disadvantage for certain U.S. mineral industries.

On this basis, the Executive Council, of the AFL-CIO called upon Congress to reject the United States-Canadian Free Trade Agreement, and we ask Congress and this committee to do so.

READING NO. 18

A CANADIAN ECONOMIST'S CASE FOR THE FTA[18]

This excerpt from the introduction to John Crispo's book is probably the single most coherent of the Canadian arguments for the FTA. John Crispo is a professor in the School of Management of the University of Toronto.

γ   γ   γ

The case for free trade with the United States is very strong for a mixture of theoretical and practical reasons. On the theoretical side the arguments pertaining to comparative advantage, economies of scale, and consumer sovereignty remain as valid as ever.

Although neglected in the public debate in Canada over free trade, the importance of comparative advantage is unassailable. This is the economic principle that shows that if every country concentrates on the production of goods and services that it can produce relatively more efficiently than other countries, national and world living standards will be maximized. Therefore, in the case of both Canada and the United States it pays each country to specialize in those goods and services that it can produce comparatively cheaper than the other.

More ready and secure access to the U.S. market will allow Canadian producers to specialize more than they have in the past. With economies of scale, this specialization should permit them to become more competitive not only in North America but also in the world at large. By gearing up to exploit the U.S. markets, Canadian producers will be better preparing themselves to take on even more competitive off-shore producers.

[18] John Crispo, "Introduction," in John Crispo, ed., *Free Trade, The Real Story*. Toronto: Gage Educational Publishing, 1988, 2–5.

Consumer sovereignty is obviously enhanced by specialization, since this allows consumers in both countries a wider range of choices at lower prices. This is a much-neglected advantage of the free-trade debate in Canada, which explains why the Consumers' Association of Canada is a firm supporter of the FTA. In the long run, no group stands to gain more from free trade than consumers.

Of more immediate concern are three other pragmatic arguments for free trade with the United States, related to the theoretical ones previously highlighted. These pragmatic arguments fall into that may be described as negative, neutral, and positive categories. The negative argument goes to the heart of the real choice that confronts Canada in terms of its trading relations with the United States.

Many Canadians have been misled into believing that the real choice is between free trade and the status quo. . . .

The problem is that the real choice confronting Canada in terms of its trading relations with the United States is not between free trade and the status quo. It is between free trade and growing U.S. protectionism. Exposure to any version of the U.S. omnibus trade bill should be enough to appall any Canadian.

People in southern Ontario have even more to fear from the threatened gutting of the auto pact that is almost certain to occur without the FTA. In addition there are literally hundreds of other industry-specific protectionist bills lurking about in the U.S. Congress.

The neutral pragmatic argument for the Canada-U.S. FTA relates to the other options that are available to Canada. Anti-free traders usually cite the General Agreement on Tariffs and Trade (GATT) as the alternative on which Canada should rely.

The GATT has served Canada well since World War II and Canadians who believe in free trade also believe in the GATT. Indeed, the two are quite complementary since the Canada-U.S. FTA is consistent with the GATT.

The problem with the GATT from a Canadian point of view is that it is on a four- to five-year negotiating timetable. That is too long for Canada to wait, given the imminent threat of more U.S. protectionism. Furthermore, there is precious little assurance of a GATT breakthrough.

This is because the United States is quite legitimately insisting that other countries reduce their agricultural and service sector barriers if the United States is not to raise its manufacturing barriers. Canada fully supports this U.S. demand, particularly in relation to agricultural commodities. The problem is that powerful vested interests—particularly among farmers in western Europe and Japan—may be too strong to permit these countries to make the kinds of concessions that are required.

The advantage of free trade with the United States for Canada is twofold in the GATT context. In the first place it provides an example for the world that could help to break the GATT logjam. At the same time it provides a hedge against any possible breakdown in the GATT negotiations.

The positive case for free trade with the United States should be obvious. The United States represents the single wealthiest market on the face of the earth. More ready and secure access to that market can provide Canada with an opportunity that will be the envy of the rest of the world. This is all the more important since Canada does not appear to have the competitive strength to export large volumes of manufactured goods to any other country.

The latter point undermines the argument that free trade will turn Canadians into hewers of wood and drawers of water. The reverse is actually the case, since the United States is the only country to which Canada now exports a significant amount of manufactured goods. Even if the United States is deemed to represent an economy in secular decline—an unsubstantiated claim at best—it will remain a lucrative market for Canadian producers for the foreseeable future.

The arguments in favor of free trade with the United States are basically economic in nature but they have obvious non-economic ramifications. This is because it is only through the economic growth and prosperity that free trade can help produce that Canada can generate the wherewithal to finance more generous cultural, regional-development, and social-security programs.

Most of those who favor the FTA feel just as strongly about these programs as anyone else. Unlike many others, however, they worry about how these programs are to be paid for, particularly if Canada loses any more access for its products and services to its major foreign market than it already has.

READING NO. 19

THE CANADIAN BUSINESS COMMUNITY'S CASE FOR THE FTA[19]

The following excerpt comes from a supplement to the major Canadian dailies which the main business lobby group, the Canadian Alliance for Trade and Job Opportunities, paid for on November 10, 1988, that is during the Canadian election campaign.

γ   γ   γ

What it is. The Free-Trade Agreement is a commercial arrangement that begins and ends with trade. It is about tariffs and other barriers at the border. It is about increasing trade and job opportunities. Most important of all, it is about fair rules in the trade game with our largest trading partner.

It does not affect our sovereignty. It does not harm our social programs. It does not menace our health care programs. It does not undermine our culture. It does not threaten our environment, our fresh water, our energy resources or our farmers. Any claims to the contrary are false. They are not based on the facts of the agreement. They are based on fear.

Most of all, it is not a sell-out. It is an opportunity. Canada is not and will not become a colony of the United States. Canada is and will remain a free, vibrant and independent nation.

So who needs it, anyway? We do. Canada is a nation that was built on trade. More than 3 million jobs depend on trade. Two out of every three of those jobs rely on trade with the United States. We need more open and secure access to a large market. We are the only industrialized country that does not have such access. The United States market is the richest and most dynamic market in the world. And it is Canada's most important

---

[19]"Straight Talk on Free Trade," *The Toronto Star*, November 10, 1988 (Supplement).

market. Without the FTA, that market is neither free nor secure and our future will be uncertain.

But three-quarters of our trade is already free of tariffs. Yes and No. While many of our products enter duty free, many more are not sold at all because of high tariffs. Thousands of products continue to attract tariffs. And it is hard to compete when you have to pay high tariffs—such as the 18% tariff on petrochemicals, or the 33% tariff on woven fabrics. It is mostly raw materials that are free while finished goods continue to draw tariffs. Getting rid of these tariffs means more opportunities to sell manufactured goods and more such opportunities mean more and better jobs. . . .

O.K. So what's in it for me? More jobs. Better jobs. More wealth to improve government services such as day-care. And direct personal benefits. You'll find that the average food bill for a family of four will go down about $100 a year—about one week's grocery bill. That's just for starters. There will also be a much larger selection of goods at lower prices on our shelves (just like across the border). For example the 20%–25% tariffs we place on U.S. shoes, baby clothes, dresses, sheets and pillowcases will be gradually eliminated.

In addition, Canadians looking to buy and furnish a new house can expect a saving of up to $8,000 as a result of tariff removal. And almost 3/4 of the new jobs created under free trade will be in the service sector of our economy where most young men and women are now employed.

While the border will not be erased, eliminating these tariff barriers will increase competition. In a nutshell, the agreement will bring benefits right across this country by opening new doors to our products and services, reducing costs for consumers, attracting new capital investment, stimulating technological innovation, creating jobs and helping to end regional disparity. . . .

I've heard we're selling out our sovereignty, along with our environment, health care, water supply, energy and culture in order to get the deal. Have you ever noticed that the people who tell you we're about to lose all this never point out specific clauses in the agreement to support their claims? The reason is simple. They're wrong. There are no such clauses.

The environment is a good example. In Canada the primary responsibility for environmental protection is with the provincial governments. But the agreement does not touch their jurisdiction at all (Chapter Six, Article 601). In addition, under the agreement the federal government maintains its full sovereign powers to take any measures "whose purpose is to protect health, safety, essential security, the environment or consumer interests" (Chapter Six, Articles 603 and 609). So there's nothing at risk. . . .

You haven't said a word about how this will stop American protectionism. Don't their trade laws still apply to everything we do? Under the agreement *both* Canada and the U.S. maintain their current trade laws, in accordance with the GATT. However, we know that U.S. protectionism won't go away with a wish and a prayer. That's why we need this agreement.

When you're playing the game with someone 10 times your size it's good to have some rules you both agree on. A referee for when you don't is also a must. That's what we've arranged. The binding dispute settlement process, in which Canada has equal voice to the U.S., prevents politically motivated application of trade laws (exactly what happened in the softwood lumber case).

We also have secured strict limits on American use of import quotas that hurt industries like steel. Finally, we now have the right to challenge proposed new trade laws before the U.S. can spring them on us and then have a bi-national panel to decide whether they are fair ball or not consistent with this agreement or the GATT.

READING NO. 20A

THE CANADIAN CONSERVATIVE PARTY'S ARGUMENTS FOR THE FTA[20A]

On December 15, 1987, just after the terms of the FTA became known, The Toronto Star *published the views of the leaders of the three major Canadian political parties. Prime Minister Brian Mulroney's Progressive Conservative Party was the only one of the three which favored the Agreement.*

γ   γ   γ

Prime Minister Brian Mulroney says the free trade deal gives Canadians the opportunity to compete on fair and equal terms, under impartially administered rules, in the world's richest market. Here is his statement on free trade.

I'm happy to have this opportunity to share with The Star and its readers my thoughts on the free trade agreement, and why I believe it will be good for Metro, good for Ontario, and good for all of Canada.

Quite simply, I believe the agreement presents Canadians with new opportunities for prosperity and new challenges to make our economy more competitive.

I want our products to be known for their excellence, our people to be celebrated for their innovative skills.

For the free trade agreement does not mean we can sit back and watch the world come to us. On the contrary, it means we must go out and aggressively seek and conquer new markets.

Any why is that? Because the United States is the biggest, richest market in the world. If Canadians can be known for their excellence and dynamism in the U.S., there is nowhere our products and expertise will not be in demand.

[20A]*The Toronto Star*, December 15, 1987.

This is a call to collective excellence. We are saying to Canadians, let us dare to be the best.

There is no doubt in my mind about the answer of Canadians. Our people do not shrink from such challenges, we welcome them.

There is no free ride here, and no free lunch. But there is an opportunity to compete on fair and equal terms, on a level field, by agreed rules that will be impartially administered.

To those who say Canadians can't compete in U.S. markets, I say we are already competing there, and holding our own. Is it not Canadians such as the Reichmann brothers and Mort Zuckerman who are adding a new dimension to the Manhattan skyline? Is it not Northern Telecom, of Mississauga, that has aggressively moved into U.S. markets to become a world tele-communications giant? Doesn't Torstar's own paperback division, Harlequin, do very well in the United States?

To those who say our industry will go into decline without the protection of the tariff walls, I say have confidence in the quality and competitiveness of Canadian products.

There will be adjustments in some sectors, such as the wine and grape industry in Ontario. But government is there to help affected industries and workers with the transition. And Canadians are already one of the most mobile work forces in the world. More than four million Canadians, about one-third of our work force, change jobs every year.

It is a balanced agreement, good for both countries, a win-win.

There is a part of some Canadians' mind set that finds it difficult to believe or accept that we could negotiate a good deal with the Americans.

I suppose they would have to listen to what some American legislators and lobbyists have been saying to the contrary—that we did too well.

Israel, which has a free trade agreement with the U.S., would like its agreement upgraded to match some of the elements of our deal. The Koreans and the Japanese and the Asian nations would like to achieve similar access.

I appreciate that there are those who disagree with us. But I believe that the agreement is very much in Ontario's interest, and very much in the national interest.

And in the bipartisan spirit of this issue I welcome the support of former trade minister Gerald Regan, who stated: "The greatest assurance of protection of our sovereignty, and our culture, is the maintenance of a strong economy. Free trade, with the greatest market on earth, gives us an opportunity to strengthen our economy that any other country on earth would give their eye teeth to have."

I believe the free trade agreement will create new opportunities for Ontario and I hope the Government of Ontario will identify those opportunities. I am confident that the economy of Ontario and all of Canada will continue to flourish under the free trade agreement.

We want a country renowned for its competitive excellence. A country on the leading edge of the new technologies.

A country capable of creating interesting jobs for our youth, and lasting prosperity for their tomorrows. A country where working women achieve full equality and dignity.

A country celebrated for its economic achievements and its social compassion. A country that is open to the world. A country, in short, that is prepared for the challenges of the coming years.

A country that is united, prosperous, sovereign and strong. A country called Canada. A model of tolerance and prosperity among the nations of the earth.

READING NO. 20B

THE CANADIAN LIBERAL PARTY'S ARGUMENTS AGAINST THE FTA[20B]

John Turner's Liberal Party formed the Official Opposition in the Canadian House of Commons. He and his party opposed the FTA not on ideological grounds, but because they saw it as a bad deal.

γ   γ   γ

Liberal leader John Turner says the Mulroney government acted on incorrect assumptions to reach a free trade deal with the U.S. Here, in a statement issued by his office last week, is Turner's position on free trade.

The free trade deal will profoundly change this country. There is no mandate for this deal. It was not discussed in the last general election. I will oppose it, up to and during a federal election.

The Mulroney government went into the trade negotiations with the United States with three naive assumptions—assumptions shared by many who support this deal:

First, that the very fact of obtaining a trade agreement would somehow exempt us from protectionist pressures in the U.S.— particularly the pressures in the U.S. Congress. Those who support the deal say that without it, we are going to be subject to American protectionist pressures and we are going to be discriminated against in our efforts to export into the U.S. market.

We would have only gained exemption from that protectionist sentiment if we had gained an exemption from American trade law. We have not. That we would was the first naive assumption.

[20B]*The Toronto Star*, December 15, 1987.

The second naive assumption was that somehow we could get a "quick fix"—we could get a quick deal with the United States. But we have always done better in lowering trade barriers with the U.S. when we dealt internationally. We have moved through the Kennedy Round and the Tokyo Round of GATT and, because of our over-all dealings with the Third World and Europe and Japan and the U.S., we were able to successfully lower the trade barriers between our two countries so that already—without this deal—about 85 per cent of everything we move across the American border moves free of duty.

The Mulroney government thought that they could get a quick fix by going head-to-head with the strongest economic power in the world when this government politically wanted a deal more than the U.S. wanted it. As a result, if you want the deal more than the other fellow, and he is 10 times stronger, you get a lousy deal. And we got a lousy deal.

The third naive assumption is that the U.S. really wants a free trade deal, which isn't true. The U.S. has always wanted fair trade, reciprocal trade, the level playing field. And that means their rules, their line, their goalposts, their ball, their uniforms—and four downs!

Supporters say we need secure access. For Canada to have gained secure access into the U.S. market, we needed two conditions:

☐ a specific exemption to American trade law.
☐ a binding dispute settlement mechanism to settle disputes between our two countries based on a neutral law.

We have got neither in this trade agreement. The dispute settlement mechanism is just a review panel, and it may not even be constitutional in the U.S. because it side-steps the American court system.

But this review panel has the power only to apply American law and American trade practice to Canadian exports. Its only review jurisdiction is to decide whether American trade tribunals have correctly applied American law. It hasn't got the right to challenge the validity of American law as we can under the General Agreement on Tariffs and Trade.

Without the trade deal, we had two appeal routes: one through the U.S. courts and one through GATT. Under this deal, we must choose one route or the other—not both.

Any agreement which did not contain a binding dispute mechanism and a binding exemption from U.S. trade law wouldn't be worth the paper it is written on.

Mulroney now says he has achieved that objective, but it isn't so. We continue to be bound by American trade law.

This is a selective trade agreement.

Some industries are in; some are out. The breweries escaped. The wine industry is caught. The B.C. and Ontario wine industries are crippled. Communications is out. Textiles are in. Agriculture is in. Procurement is mostly out.

You don't have to get into a philosophical discussion about free trade—you just have to examine the deal like any other contract. What did we get? And what did we give away? We didn't get secure access and we gave away too much.

Moreover, this is not just a trade deal. It goes beyond trade-related items. It virtually eliminates our screening process for foreign investment. We lost our capital markets—banks can now be owned by Americans.

This is a "Sale of Canada Act!" It is the most massive sell-out of Canadian economic independence and sovereignty in our history.

Mulroney tells us that in opposing his deal, we are "timid" and "fearful" and "don't have confidence in Canada." He is dead wrong.

We do have confidence in Canada—confidence in our future. But it is not a continental future. It is a Canadian future.

READING NO. 20C

THE CANADIAN NEW DEMOCRATIC PARTY'S ARGUMENTS AGAINST THE FTA[20C]

Ed Broadbent's New Democratic Party, a social democratic party, opposed the FTA on practical as well as ideological grounds.

γ   γ   γ

New Democratic party leader Ed Broadbent says the free trade deal puts hundreds of thousands of Canadian jobs at risk, and that the Prime Minister should call an election on the issue. Here is his statement on free trade.

The Mulroney trade deal truly jeopardizes our country's future. I believe that the more Canadians learn about this deal, the more they will demand it be torn up.

During the last election campaign, the Prime Minister promised more honesty and fairness. Since the election, whether you consider promises to pensioners, tax fairness or fairness for Canada's regions, he has done the exact opposite. Now we have the greatest betrayal of all—the Mulroney trade deal.

Canadians should remember this government's track record when listening to the Conservatives' trade deal promises.

What does this trade deal mean?

It means lost jobs. Hundreds of thousands of Canadian jobs are at risk. Our families, our neighbors and our communities will suffer the consequences. One Mulroney cabinet minister estimated the deal could put as many as 500,000 people out of work.

It means extra hardships for women. More than 80 per cent of women in the labor force work in banks, health services,

[20C]*The Toronto Star*, December 15, 1987.

telecommunications and administration, areas that will be the most directly affected.

It means companies could pick up and move south of the border, where there are weaker worker health and safety laws, weaker environmental laws and no programs such as medicare.

We have given up our right to make sure foreign investment helps instead of hurts our country. Virtually every Canadian company is open to unrestricted takeover.

This government cannot deny the facts: Canadian businesses create far more jobs for Canadians than U.S.-controlled companies. Recently, Statistics Canada disclosed that for every $1 billion in profits, Canadian companies created 5,700 new jobs between 1978 and 1985. For the same $1 billion of profits during the same period, U.S. firms created a grand total of 17 jobs in Canada.

Brian Mulroney's trade deal guts the Auto Pact, jeopardizing thousands of Canadian jobs. Gone are the tariff penalties that kick in if manufacturers do not meet a minimum level of Canadian content or production ratios based on the number of cars sold in Canada.

The Mulroney trade deal means more pain for Canada's farmers. The deal will hurt the family farmer and lead to lost jobs and lower returns for agricultural producers. All agricultural tariffs will be phased out. The elimination of tariffs on processed foods will cost Canadian farmers a huge share of the Canadian market.

The U.S. can sell us even more chicken, turkey, grain, eggs, egg products and processed foods. It is estimated that increased U.S. chicken imports alone will cost Canadian farmers $21 million.

Mulroney has handed over to U.S. President Ronald Reagan complete access to Canadian energy. The result: If we suffer an energy crisis, Canada won't be able to meet its own needs first.

The deal will limit our ability to productively use our natural resources to help diversify the Canadian economy, particularly in the West. For example, before the deal we could sell our oil and gas to Canadian petrochemical companies at cheaper prices than their U.S. competitors. Under this deal, we can't do that. This simple effective step to make our country more competitive is taken away from us.

The Conservatives promised our ability to promote regional fairness would not be touched. By now, some government officials admit this isn't true. They admit this trade deal limits our control over our own economic strategies. It threatens our regional development and social programs which are viewed by some American business interests as unfair subsidies.

To top it off, Canadians do not gain secure access to U.S. markets. The dispute settlement procedure that Mulroney said was his "bottom line" will not decide whether a U.S. retaliatory action was unfair; it will only decide whether existing U.S. law has been properly applied. All existing powers of the U.S. Congress to take unfair action when we win the competition, as they did with softwood, will remain in place.

I am fighting this deal because I have confidence in our ability to compete as an independent country. Mulroney and the Conservatives do not have a mandate to change the face of Canada, as we know it, forever.

Canadians did not vote for this trade deal in 1984. It was not discussed in a single speech in the last election campaign. In fact, Mulroney campaigned against free trade in the 1983 Tory leadership race.

We must make it clear to this government that it is our right to have a say in a decision affecting our future, our children's future and their children's future. Mulroney should call an election now.

READING NO. 21

A FAMOUS CANADIAN NOVELIST
OPPOSES THE FTA[21]

Margaret Atwood, a Canadian novelist who has won world-wide recognition, first wrote this piece for the book, If You Love This Country. *(Laurier LaPierre, ed., Toronto: McClelland and Stewart, 1987) This revised version, appropriately entitled "On Being Canadian," was published in the magazine of the Canadian Union of Public Employees.*

γ   γ   γ

I would dearly like to hope this trade agreement is going to be in some way good for the country. Why? Partly because it is Canadian to take that attitude. As a nation we do tend to have this touching and naive belief that those in authority know what they are doing; but also because if someone comes along and puts their hand over your eyes and shoves an unknown substance down your throat, all you have got to fall back on is hope. You just hope like heck it is going to turn out to be good for you in the end.

So I am sitting around reading the rhetoric in the newspapers with my ears aflap for good news, open to being convinced, but so far I am not.

I would like to share with you some of the reasons why not and put to you some of the questions that trouble my waking hours, and even my sleeping hours during which Dief the Chief appears to me in dreams, jowls quivering in outrage, and asks me what is going on and why the prime minister began by saying that free trade would threaten Canada's sovereignty but changed his mind after the election, while Sir John A. Macdonald revolves rapidly in his grave.

[21]Margaret Atwood, "On Being Canadian," *The Facts* (CUPE), X:2 (Spring 1988), 13–14.

No hard facts

Do not ask me, ask them, I say. But ghosts have a way of visiting only those who remember them. My first worry is that there are no hard facts. Why not? For the simple reason that nobody can predict the future. Witness Black Monday last October. No matter how many graphs you draw up, as long as they are graphs about the future they do not necessarily hold any more water than a leaky boot.

The future is like life after death: you can say anything you like about it because nobody can actually go there and come back and tell us about it.

We know more or less what we are giving up, though we will not know the whole of it until after the fine print has been passed through the mental digestive systems of the lawyers, but we cannot know what we are getting in return. In short, I do not understand the full scope and implications of this agreement and I do not believe anybody else really does either. Maybe I am just stupid; if so, there are a lot more stupid people like me running around loose.

We are told that the polls show a 49%-in-favour response. But I distrust poll results. Why? Because I have a background in market research and I know the answers you get depend a lot on how you ask the questions. I expect that if the poll question is simply "Are you in favour of free trade?" you are going to get a certain amount of "yes" because free is a positive word, as a free gift, free lunch, free world and free speech.

But if you asked "Are you in favour of this particular trade deal if it means you have to give up your health insurance, unemployment benefits and regional development aid—which remain vulnerable to challenge as unfair subsidies under U.S. trade law—and if you also have to give up Canada's foreign affairs autonomy and our visibility in arts and entertainment, and if it also means we are committed to playing only by the other guy's rules," I expect you would get a different response.

A level playing-field

And what if you asked "Are you in favour of this deal if it means the disintegration of Canada?" Maybe that is something we should ask. In other words, do we really want a country? A level playing field, after all, is one from which all distinguishing features have been removed. . . .

Canada as a separate but dominated country has done about as well under the United States as women world-wide have done under men. About the only position they have ever adopted toward us, country to country, has been the missionary position, and we were not on top. I guess that is why the national wisdom vis-a-vis them has so often taken the form of lying still, keeping your mouth shut, and pretending you like it. But, as part of them, at least we get to vote. We would sure as heck fit in. We already know more about them than we know about one another, or so you would think.

It is no use ridiculing scenarios like this or calling people who talk about them cowards or idiots or Nazis or self-interested, all of which terms have been bandied about recently—just as it is no good calling pro-free-traders cowards or idiots or Nazis or self-interested. It is no good accusing people of wrapping themselves in the flag.

I might point out in passing that it seems to be okay in the States to do this flag-waving act. They have this thing called patriotism. It is thought of as standing up for yourself. But in Canada it is seen as bad taste, or even subversive. I wonder why.

May I suggest that instead of name-calling each side should try to find out what will really be "good for the country." This throws us back to Philosophy 101. How do you define "good"? Is it only money we are talking about here? I do not think so. Canadian people, like people everywhere, have values other than money that are important to them. Their fears of losing those values are real fears, by which I mean that they are truly held and must be addressed.

A chance of surviving

It is no use claiming that there is some mysterious gene of Canadianness welded into us at conception that will guarantee the retention of these values even if all the social structures, educational underpinnings and cultural manifestations of them disappear.

What will be done, if anything, to give these values a fighting chance of surviving? As George Bernard Shaw commented when a beautiful actress wanted to have a child with him so it would have her looks and his brains, "But, madam, what if it has *my* looks and *your* brains?" We would like to think we are about to get the best of both worlds—Canadian stability and a more caring society, along with American markets, but what if instead we get their crime rate, health programs and gun laws, and they get our markets—or what is left of them?

It is no use saying that this is mere anti-Yankee paranoia. A lot of us get along just fine in the country of superlatives; as for myself, it is the land of my ancestors and the haunt of my youth. It is not about liking the great *them*; it is about wanting to be who *you* are.

Anyone from Quebec understands the connection between culture, society and politics, although others sometimes have to have it spelled out. Short form: just because you like women does not mean you want to be one.

It is no use saying that these are emotional arguments, as if that disqualifies them. Almost all of the arguments heard so far in this debate have been emotional arguments. Fear is an emotion, yes, and love of country is an emotion—but greed is an emotion, too. . . .

Mercury is the god of exchange and money, but he is not the god of gifts. He does not make something-for-nothing deals. There is always a price. "Is it free?" is not a real question when you are dealing with the god of trade. The only appropriate question is whether the price is too high. Well, is it?

Dealing with the devil

. . . The other notable deal-maker in folklore is the devil. He never offers give-aways, either. His usual deal is your soul in exchange for the promise of future wealth. But he is even trickier to deal with than Mercury is, because in a typical devil's bargain you end up with neither. The only defence against such "bargains" is the exercise of the seven cardinal virtues, which for those who cannot immediately recall them to mind are faith, hope, charity, fortitude, temperance, justice, and prudence.

Prudence is what you should exercise when buying a life insurance policy, which apparently this deal is intended to be. Prudence means reading the fine print very carefully.

If we end up in a situation where the Americans are virtually our only trading partner, and they have so much more economic clout over us, we are really not just the tail of the dog, but the very end of the tail of the dog. We are going to be whipped around whenever that tail wags.

I wish all Canadians a lot of luck, because as a country we are going to need it.

READING NO. 22

LLOYD AXWORTHY SUMMARIZES THE CASE AGAINST THE FTA[22]

In this presentation to a seminar at McGill University, Lloyd Axworthy, the Liberal Party's main spokesperson on the FTA, opposes the Agreement with reference to its specific features.

γ γ γ

. . . The one other country which is currently negotiating a free trade agreement with the U.S. has said it would never accept the conditions Canada has accepted. Specifically, Mexico has said its energy resources are its own and will not necessarily be shared in times of crisis with the Americans.

In specific sectors, Canada has paid an enormous cost. The horticultural industries, with a clearly shorter growing season, must now face the phasing out of tariffs over a period of years. Communities in the Niagara Peninsula and Okanogan will face severe hardship. Already, grape growers are discovering that banks will loan no money without collateral from another source.

Many firms in the Montreal area who manufacture textiles will also face liquidation shortly. The cost here is in real human lives and must be accounted for by this government, which still refuses to admit that adjustment programs for such workers should have been an essential part of any free trade agreement. Mike Wilson tells us the market place will handle the adjustment.

[22]Lloyd Axworthy, "Free Trade—The Costs for Canada," in A.R. Riggs and Tom Velk, eds., *Canadian-American Free Trade: (The Sequel). Historical, Political and Economic Dimensions*, Halifax: Institute for Research on Public Policy, 1988, 37–39.

The auto industry in Canada has lost its safeguards and incentives for off shore investment. Several autoparts firms have threatened to move to the U.S. because of the free trade deal. Thousands of jobs are at risk in the autoparts industries. . . .

Throw into that mix the concessions already made in terms of the NEP, FIRA and countless political confrontations with the Americans from drilling rights in the Beaufort Sea to American submarines in Canadian waters.

These are the immediate costs of Free Trade and they greatly outweigh the benefits. What is of far greater significance is the power we have lost as a nation to shape our political-economy and thereby our national destiny. Despite the fact this deal is a bad one on the basis of its own economic merits, it also represents a new and unsettling direction for Canada.

As the Hon. Mitchell Sharp said before the Parliamentary committee,

From the very beginnings of our country, we have sought to preserve a separate identity, to live in harmony with our next-door neighbour but as an independent country. By entering into this bilateral, preferential agreement, we would be deciding no longer to resist the continental pull. On the contrary, we would be accelerating the process of the Americanization of Canada.

"The Americanization of Canada," what does that phrase mean, for I believe it gets to the heart of the Free Trade issue. It can be defined as the elevation of the invisible hand of the market to the level of a deity. It means the gradual erosion of Canada's political economy, that unique historical mixture of government and private industry forging a nation and solving its problems together for an economy driven exclusively by the forces of a continental market.

It means increased harmonization of economic and social policies and limitation of the basic tools of political decision-making used for generations to build this nation.

Donald Smiley, noted Canadian constitutional scholar puts it well. He says,

The free trade proposal challenges the fundamentals of Canada's nationhood . . . Canada is preeminently a political notion and what its citizens share is a common set of governmental institutions. National and sub-national governments have used their powers in pursuit of a wide variety of purposes. Such powers are limited by the circumstances of interdependence and in particular by the domination of foreign multinationals. Despite these constraints, Canadian governments have in respect to many matters established policies differing from those of the United States.

It is this range of freedom of action which supporters of free trade would have Canadians surrender. As a result, we are foreclosing our own future.

Mr. Mulroney and his allies have said the reason for a comprehensive free trade deal is jobs. The government has yet to provide any clear evidence to support their claims. Constant reference to the Economic Council Report no longer has relevance, as their computer simulation does not include some key variables—the continuation of trade remedy laws and the inclusion of services. And, as we have been warned there could be serious job losses in this area.

Equally misleading are the assertions that free trade automatically leads to higher growth and productivity. One can ask why it is that the United States in the 1970's had a .8% increase in productivity even though they had access to a huge market. Or, why many European countries experienced high unemployment or low growth, even as members of the Common Market. In other words there is no automatic guarantee of economic success.

Another proposition that the proposed deal would seriously undermine is our ability to achieve full employment. It is useful to look at the work of Gortan Therborn, a Dutch professor who analyzed the fifteen top industrial countries, including Canada, to see why some were successful in creating full employment and others were not. His conclusions were that the factors that made a difference were not ideology, growth rates, deficit reduction or export performance. The first essential ingredient was a commitment to full employment that was integral to the various economic structures of the country, and therefore influenced economic decision making.

To make this commitment work, there must be sufficient

independence to allow governments to make the necessary choices, design the appropriate blueprints, have the required flexibility to adopt and alter policies according to the given circumstances. There must be the freedom to choose the right mix of fiscal, monetary, labour market, tariff, investment, development policies to maximize the possibilities of full employment.

If one were to follow this analysis, the Canadian government rather than aiming for greater integration of our economy should be striving for greater independence. So, when and if there is a readiness in Canada to truly implement a full employment policy, then we will be able to do so. And I can testify that it is possible, as a former minister of employment I had prepared such a plan for the previous government.

But under the Mulroney deal future government will have fewer public policy instruments, fewer choices, and will be far more dependent on a continental economy.

This agreement has limited our ability to use both regional specific public policies and the comparative advantage in our energy sector; it has given up essential infrastructural support programs such as those currently in use in the transportation and telecommunication sectors; and it has limited our capacity to foster emerging, infant industries in high technology.

We may also be running the risk of cutting off alternative trade options and opportunities. The last three years have seen a precipitous drop in our exports to the Pacific Rim, Latin America and Europe.

A U.S. trade deal that discriminates against third countries could yield even further trade diversion away from Canada. As our economy becomes even more foreign dominated the opportunities for export mandates will be limited—out ability to develop public investment policies circumscribed.

So I would say to you our freedom of action is not some bleeding heart concern. It is a deep-set concern about the loss of our right to nation build and pursue liberal minded policies in the future.

If our objective is full employment and an end to regional

disparity then we must maintain, indeed restore, vitality to the public economy of Canada. It is not the market that should determine Canada's future, but a market place working in partnership with effective public policies to achieve a future of economic vitality and national equity.

READING NO. 23

PRESIDENT BUSH REVIEWS THE IMPLEMENTATION OF THE FTA[23]

The Free Trade Agreement implementation legislation requires the President to make a report to Congress every two years. The following extract is taken from the introduction of the first of these biennial reports.

γ   γ   γ

Implementation of the FTA has proceeded smoothly over the past two years. . . .The many bilateral institutional mechanisms of the FTA have proven useful in resolving a number of issues before they could become serious disputes. The outlook is for further growth as the staged removal of impediments continues during the ten-year phase-in period.

. . . In 1989 U.S. shipments to Canada accounted for more than 20 percent of the value of all U.S. exports of merchandise, and nearly equalled our exports to all EC countries combined.

Given the significance of our relationship with Canada and the scope of the FTA, there were remarkably few disputes that arose during the first two years of implementation. . . .The provisions for binational review of final determination under national antidumping and countervailing duty laws have been implemented in a responsible manner. . . .

. . . Probably the most notable success in term of trade liberalization . . . is the agreement . . . to accelerate elimination of duties. . . .

While the United States and Canada have made some progress in certain issues such as the effort to reach a common

---

[23]*The United States-Canada Free-Trade Agreement. Biennial Report.* A Report from the President to the Congress under Section 304(f) of the United States-Canada Free Trade Agreement Implementation Act. [Washington]: January 1991, pp. 1–3.

187

performance standard for certain plywood, in other areas there has been less progress than we would have preferred. It is disappointing, for example, that Canada has not agreed to increase the required value content requirement of the rule of origin for automotive products. . . .

With respect to some . . . issues, such as investment, agriculture, subsidies, intellectual property rights and services, both the United States and Canada have focussed their respective negotiating efforts on the multilateral trade negotiations under the Uruguay Round. As the latter negotiations draw to a conclusion, we will be evaluating the results and pursuing the possibilities for further progress on a bilateral basis.

Another avenue through which further U.S.-Canadian cooperation on trade is being pursued involves a potential Free Trade Agreement linking, the U.S., Mexico and Canada. Canada is currently involved in exploratory discussions with the U.S. and Mexico to determine whether there is a basis for Canadian participation in negotiations on the schedule proposed for the U.S.-Mexico FTA.

. . . With a shared commitment to the FTA and continued hard work, the United States and Canada stand to improve further upon this mutually beneficial relationship.

READING NO. 24

THE CANADIAN GOVERNMENT REVIEWS THE IMPLEMENTATION OF THE FTA[24]

In March 1991, the government of Canada published the second annual report on the implementation of the Canada-United States Free Trade Agreement. The following reading is taken from the summary and the introduction to the report. This report is more positive than the U.S. report summarized in Reading 23, probably because the FTA is more controversial in Canada than in the United States and the government would, therefore, prefer not to admit to problems.

γ   γ   γ

The FTA is working well and contributing to a more positive trading relationship with the United States. Its implementation in 1990 proceeded in a smooth and effective manner and no significant difficulties have been encountered. . . .

The Co-Chairmen of the Auto Select Panel recommended that the FTA North American value-added requirement be raised from 50 to 60%, but Canada indicated that it would not consider increasing the content rule unless it clearly benefited Canadian industry and improved its competitiveness. . . .

The dispute settlement mechanisms are working well and should be regarded as one of the major benefits of the FTA. Canadian interests, both industry and government, are making effective use of them. . . .

The FTA is working successfully to secure Canadian market access against U.S. protectionist measures. Some examples of how the FTA preserved Canadian market access in 1990 are the following:

---

[24]External Affairs and International Trade Canada. Free Trade Management Division. *Free Trade News. Implementation and Issues Update*. Ottawa: March 1991.

- A bill to restrict the import of textiles and footwear specifically exempted Canada from the proposed trade restrictions because of the FTA. In the end, the bill was vetoed but the point is that the FTA had offered special protection to Canada.

- Legislation imposing new certification requirements for industrial fasteners (U.S. Fastener Quality Act) was modified so that Canadian fasteners are treated in the same way as U.S. fasteners. This change was critical to Canadian steel producers' ability to continue to make "just in time" deliveries to auto manufacturers.

- Canada obtained an exemption from the U.S. prohibition against the transport of lottery tickets through the United States. This allows Canadian exporters to ship their products to Mexico and other Latin American countries by the most economical route. . . .

- By relying upon the FTA, Canada was able to maintain full national treatment for the pricing of gas exports to Northern California when the California Public Utilities Commission proposed the introduction of discriminatory requirements.

- The FTA was instrumental in persuading the U.S. Small Business Administration to allow Canadian-owned companies in the United States to maintain their eligibility for U.S. Government procurements under the Small Business Set-aside Program. . . .

The goals of the Canada-United States Free Trade Agreement (FTA) remain the same now as they were at the outset: to improve the trading relationship with the USA and to ensure more secure access to Canada's largest trading partner, accounting for over 75 percent of Canadian exports; and to stimulate Canadian competitiveness and industrial efficiency.

These goals can best be achieved through continued smooth implementation of the FTA, which calls for:

- the elimination of barriers to the bilateral trade in goods and services over a ten year phase-in period;

- the facilitation of fair competition within the free-trade area;

- the liberalization of conditions for investment;

- the establishment of effective procedures for the joint administration of the Agreement and the resolution of disputes; and
- the laying of a foundation to expand and enhance the benefits of the Agreement.

Since the FTA entered into force on January 1, 1989, Canada and the USA have worked diligently to ensure its smooth implementation.

READING NO. 25

CANADA'S ROYAL BANK ESTIMATES THE EFFECTS OF THE FREE TRADE AGREEMENT[25]

The entire February 1991 issue of the Royal Bank's monthly newsletter was devoted to the impact of the FTA on the Canadian economy. The Royal Bank is one of Canada's largest banks, and Edward Neufeld, an executive vice-president of the bank and himself an economist, was one of the FTA's most vocal defenders. The following extract is taken from the introduction and summary of the special issue.

γ   γ   γ

After two years, the effect of the Canada-U.S. free trade agreement (FTA) has been overshadowed by other economic forces, including recession, high real interest rates needed to contain inflationary pressures and the resulting strength of the Canadian dollar. However, although the economic effects of the FTA are difficult to isolate, it is important to attempt to evaluate the influence of the free trade agreement on Canada's economy, how it is interacting with other important economic forces and where it is leading us. Only through such an assessment, can government, business and labour pursue the most effective policies and strategies that will permit Canada to obtain the maximum economic benefits available from free trade.

Executive summary
Here are our main findings to date:

- The major economic development since our last review of the progress of free trade has been the onset of recession in

[25]*Econoscope*, February 1991, 2.

Canada after an historically long period of expansion, especially in the manufacturing sector.

■ The recession is made worse by high real interest rates and a high exchange rate which, in turn, are the result of years of large fiscal deficits and, in recent years, a tendency for increases in Canadian manufacturing costs to outrun those of the United States and other major trading partners.

■ Compared with the 1981–82 recession, the job losses so far in the current recession are much lower. In the first three quarters of the last recession, 264,000 jobs were lost. In the first three quarters of the current recession, employment has dropped by 154,000 jobs.

■ Our industry review shows that for most industries experiencing difficulties, the FTA has not been a major contributor to those problems. The FTA may even have moderated the impact on the recession in some industries such as mass transit systems, petrochemicals, and electronic equipment.

■ Manufacturing industries where tariff barriers have traditionally been highest, such as furniture, textiles and clothing, have made considerable adjustments. Other industries, such as the food processing industry, have faced indirect pressures from the FTA partly because of Canada's system of agricultural supply management.

■ Since 1989, there have been reports of Canadian companies shifting operations to the United States because of the FTA. While some companies have moved, others have come to Canada. There is no clear proof as yet that Canada is, on balance, losing manufacturing jobs and investment because of free trade.

■ The dispute settlement mechanism has contributed to a more orderly review of trade disputes between the two countries. More progress needs to be made on negotiating countervail and anti-dumping rules, especially since the GATT so far has failed to improve trade rulings in these areas.

■ Canadian governments need to be more aggressive in reducing budget deficits. Lower budget deficits would reduce pressures on capital markets and would allow for lower real interest rates and for a lower exchange rate. This would encourage more investment and improved job creation in a non-inflationary environment and so ease adjustment to the new freer trade environment.

READING NO. 26

THE COUNCIL OF CANADIANS FINDS THAT THE FTA HAD NEGATIVE EFFECTS ON THE CANADIAN ECONOMY[26]

The Council of Canadians, a group organized especially in order to oppose the FTA, has continued to monitor the Agreement's effects. Its reports appear about every six months. The following extracts come from its May 1991 report.

γ   γ   γ

On the advent of the commencement of new trade negotiations designed to create a new free trade pact between Canada, the United States and Mexico, the Council of Canadians has uncovered new evidence that paints a devastating picture of the damage done to Canada since the introduction of the Free Trade Agreement in January of 1989. The report card, completed at the halfway point of the Mulroney Government's five year mandate, serves as a warning to both Canadians and to Mexicans. Free Trade Part II—the Canada-U.S.-Mexico deal appears destined to inflict further damage. What's worse for Canada is that the proposed deal will likely subsume the Canada-U.S. deal and will probably remove the few safeguards, ineffective as they may be, that exist in the Canada-U.S. Free Trade Agreement. . . .

The statistics are numbing. In the first 2½ years of free trade, a mid-term analysis shows the following:

- 315,000 manufacturing jobs have disappeared or moved away from Canada.
- 151,000 jobs in the first two months of 1991 alone have also disappeared.

---

[26][Council of Canadians], FTA Report Card: A Warning to Mexico, [Ottawa], May 30, 1991, 1–4, photocopied document.

- a decline in Gross Domestic Product
- a steady increase in foreign takeovers of Canadian companies. . . .

Entire sectors of the Canadian economy are rapidly disappearing:

- textile manufacturing has dropped by 30%
- clothing manufacturing has dropped by 18%
- furniture manufacturing has dropped by 25%
- wood manufacturing has dropped by 24%
- paper products manufacturing has dropped by 13%
- steel manufacturing has dropped by almost 30%
- auto parts manufacturing has dropped by 23%

The effect on communities is overwhelming. Windsor, Ontario is losing, on average, a plant every nine days. The Alberta canola crushing business is being destroyed by free trade, according to many experts. One of the country's largest canola-crushing plants, United Oilseed Products has closed its doors. The list goes on:

- Canadian Transport Group has closed half of its Canadian operations and has shifted most of its business to its subsidiary in Livonia, Michigan.

- Caterpillar Canada closed its recently built Brampton, Ontario plant to consolidate operations in Raleigh, North Carolina. 400 people are out of work.

- United Technologies Automotive is closing its St. Thomas, Ontario plant and moving production to the U.S., throwing 319 people out of work. . . .

SOCIAL PROGRAMS

The government has abandoned job creation, raised Unemployment Insurance premiums by 24% and has cut funds for training and jobs by $100 million. Transfer payment cuts are jeopardizing the future of medicare and post-secondary education. This exists in an atmosphere of declining Government revenues, due to a declining economy and because of the harmonization with U.S. policy, as a result of the FTA. . . .

CONCLUSION

At the half-way mark of Brian Mulroney's five year mandate, this report card serves as a mid-term analysis of the deindustrialization of the Canadian economy. These figures show that the Free Trade Agreement has been a benefit only to large American companies as Canada loses control of its economy and resources. As our economy moves south, we lost not only our standard of living, but also our ability to build our own nation around our own values. Canadians and Mexicans should beware of the perils of Free Trade Part II—the North American Free Trade Agreement.

READING NO. 27

THE AMERICAN GOVERNMENT'S REASONS FOR SEEKING A TRILATERAL FREE TRADE AGREEMENT[27]

The following summary of the U.S. reasons for seeking a free trade agreement with Mexico appears to be taken from a presidential statement to Congress.

γ   γ   γ

The United States and Mexico are embarking on free trade negotiations that in conjunction with the 1988 US-Canada Free Trade Agreement, would create a North American market of more than 360 million people and an annual economy of $6 trillion. The negotiations were made possible by congressional action on May 23–24, 1991, which granted the executive branch "fast track authority" to negotiate trade agreements, including the proposed pact with Mexico.

Fast track authority allows the executive branch to present trade agreements to Congress for approval without the possibility of amending the treaty. Amendments could undercut free trade talks, because trading partners such as Mexico would have no way of knowing what changes Congress might demand in agreements already negotiated in good faith.

Despite the granting of fast track negotiating authority, Congress remains an integral part of the process. President Bush is committed to extensive consultations with Congress throughout the negotiations. Such a process is in the best interests of US and Mexican negotiators, as it helps ensure that Congress will approve the treaty and implementing legislation that the President and Congress have developed together.

The United States hopes to build upon the success of the US-

---

[27]"Gist: North American Free Trade Agreement," *U.S. Department of State Dispatch*, June 24, 1991, 454.

Canada free trade accord. Canada has asked to be part of the negotiating process with Mexico, although the Canadian government says that any potential negotiating difficulties between Canada and Mexico will in no way affect US-Mexico talks.

Goals
The negotiations seek a broad agreement to eliminate restrictions on the flow of goods, services, and investment:

- Elimination (as far as possible) of non-tariff barriers on goods and services;

- Establishment of an open investment climate; and

- Full protection of intellectual property rights (patents, copyrights, and trademarks).

Expanded Trade With Mexico
Mexico is America's third largest trading partner, with bilateral commerce of $52 billion in 1989 and $59 billion in 1990. NAFTA would lead to expanded trade with Mexico and the creation of additional jobs for US workers. It would give US exporters unrestricted access to a Mexican market of 86 million people, which may reach 100 million by the year 2000.

Mexico purchases more than two-thirds of its imports from the United States. However, Mexico still has higher trade barriers than the United States. Its average tariff duty is 10% compared with 4% in the United States, and significant Mexican non-tariff barriers remain. The United States has much to gain from the elimination or reduction of these barriers under a trade agreement. Traditional US competitive advantages—geographic, cultural, and historic links—in this important market would be further enhanced by NAFTA.

As the Mexican economy grows, a substantial part of the increased income—as much as 15%—is spent on US goods and services. Strong Mexican growth is expected because of President Salinas' economic reforms. Mexico's middle class is increasing as a percentage of the total population; this means more consumers for American products.

The United States benefits from expanded trade. For each additional $1 billion in real net exports, about 25,000 new US jobs are created. Increased exports accounted for 88% of US economic growth in 1989–90 and have helped the US economy expand out of recessions in the past.

READING NO. 28

THE MEXICAN GOVERNMENT'S REASONS FOR SEEKING A FREE TRADE AGREEMENT WITH THE UNITED STATES[28]

In his address to the Canadian House of Commons, President Salinas gave Mexico's reasons for seeking a North American free trade agreement.

γ γ γ

Mexico has a robust identity and sufficient vitality to build its own sovereign future. We therefore do not fear an encounter with the world, rather we actively seek it. To be bent on autarky would not only be Utopian, but would mean condemning ourselves to backwardness and marginalization. Our homeland is able to look out at the world and open itself up to contact with other peoples, without thereby failing to be faithful to itself, to its traditions and culture, to its values and historical *raison d'être*. We Mexicans today look towards the future and are determined to play a significant role in the coming century. . . .

The world economy is the stage of a harsh and intense competition for markets. The revolution in knowledge and technology is transforming work habits and making social relations more fluid. New centres of innovation, resources and trade are at the forefront of economic activity and are forming into blocs to profit from their comparative advantages. To have staying power in this new international arena demands changes in economic structures, openness to competition and innovation, and new forms of association both within and outside the borders of individual nations.

In view of those circumstances, Mexico has set out to make the changes needed to secure a new placement in the world

---

[28]Canada, House of Commons, *Debates,* April 8, 1991, 19178-19181.

economy and to play an active role in the political configuration of the future. . . .

Economic stability has therefore been our highest priority. From the outset we viewed it as an essential condition for ensuring the continuity and viability of the structural measures that we have implemented in order to modernize our productive plant. The main objective is to make Mexico a major exporting country: hence the urgent need to ensure greater efficiency in productive processes and over-all quality of the end product. That is why we opened up our economy to international and domestic competition. In a brief period of time, we moved from being one of the most closed developing economies to being one of the most open. We have dismantled non-tariff barriers, removing them from over 85 per cent of imports; tariffs now average 10 per cent and the highest stands at 20 per cent. We needed to encourage innovation and competition, and to take advantage of the arbitrage of foreign prices on domestic prices.

That, in turn, meant broadening and stepping up the process of deregulating large sectors of our economy and establishing more attractive conditions to encourage greater flows of foreign direct investment, on which access to new technology largely depends. . . .

Consequently, we have begun talks with Canada and the United States of America that will, in the near future, enable us to embark on negotiations leading to the signing of a trilateral free trade treaty. I am convinced that such a treaty is unquestionably the best option for the parties involved. It is an opportunity for our three nations to create a major economic zone that while respecting our cultural differences, will have the vitality to compete successfully with the European market and the Asian Pacific Rim.

Within the framework of an agreement between sovereign nations that will do away with tariff and non-tariff barriers, increase the expanded trade patterns and objectively and justly resolve differences, we can expect investment and the creation of jobs to benefit all three countries. We will also be able to find economies of scale that will not only increase the competitiveness of Canada and restore that of the United States, but also bring Mexico's competitiveness up to world levels. A new array of technological options may well open up as a result of greater specialization and diversification in production and exports. We have what is needed to translate efforts into well-being for the inhabitants of North America. . . .

Freer trade between our nations is expected to enhance the well-being of our peoples. We must not blame free trade for the conditions imposed on the productive situation by other factors. We have nothing to fear but barriers and obstacles that are intended to protect some parties from competition and, in doing so, end up destroying creativity and well-being. We must not forget that, sooner or later, such barriers have been demolished by the freedom-seeking vitality of peoples and by their demands for justice.

Distinguished members of Parliament, a free trade agreement between Canada and the United States of America is already in force. Arduous and intense negotiations preceded the signing of this agreement and now serve as valuable experience of which Mexico hopes to take advantage. Although the debate was undoubtedly intense, it was finally shown that the economic prosperity of Canada, one of the world's most important exporting countries, is closely linked to access to new markets and consequently to plans for developing a free trade in goods and services. An economy that closes itself off loses competitiveness. An economy that is skilfully opened up gains new competitive vitality.

In Mexico we share this vocation. It is with the support of our culture and our history that we are opening up to the world and to the competition for markets. We know that the path that each nation pursues cannot be other than the result of its own historic experience, of the specific circumstances of its geography and even of the resources with which nature has endowed it. In the world of today, however, comparative advantages are not inflexible—they can be built up. The circumstances of today's world oblige us to make use of all the energy, imagination and determination of Canadians and Mexicans alike in working toward the convergence of our goals, so as to take full advantage of the complementary aspects of our economies. We can share a vision of the future, based on the long term, that will heed the needs of coming generations, who deserve to live in a better world.

READING NO. 29

THE CANADIAN GOVERNMENT'S REASONS FOR PARTICIPATING IN A TRILATERAL FREE TRADE AGREEMENT[29]

The following extracts from a speech by Canada's chief negotiator for the NAFTA are taken from a lengthy and detailed statement of the Canadian government's position. Yet this major statement was left to a relatively junior official.

γ   γ   γ

The ultimate goal of these negotiations is to create a North American market free of tariffs and non-tariff barriers. The agreement would permit the free flow of goods, services and investments among the three countries. It would provide for the protection of intellectual property rights. And it would establish a fair and expeditious dispute settlement mechanism. It would create a market of 360 million people, larger than the 12 countries of the European community.

The negotiation of such a North American agreement is a continuation and extension of the Canadian government's approach to economic policy—an approach that sees increased trade linked to increased competitiveness and increased prosperity. . . .

Both countries have realized a number of benefits from the FTA, from increased investment to increased trade. Indeed, a \$4.3-billion foreign direct investment surplus last year was Canada's first such surplus in a decade. We believe a North American Free Trade Agreement will add to the gains of the FTA. For Canada, the effects of a North American agreement

[29]External Affairs and International Trade Canada, Notes for an Address by John M. Weekes, Canada's Chief Negotiator for a North American Free Trade Agreement to the Council of the Americas and the Canadian Manufactuers' Association, Toronto, June 3, 1991.

will not be as significant as those of the FTA. But, moderate though its impact will be, it will add positively to Canada's economic performance.

The immediate benefits of an open Mexican market for Canadian exporters may be modest. But as Mexico grows, as increased trade translates into increased prosperity for Mexican workers, then I think Canadian exporters will be busy trying to keep pace with what will probably become North America's fastest growing market. Even now there are important business opportunities to be found in telecommunications, transportation, oil drilling and exploration equipment, and pollution control and abatement technology. Canadian exporters will also find opportunities in agricultural, consumer and automotive goods.

Perhaps more importantly, the creation of a trilateral market with a combined Gross Domestic Product of US$6 trillion will allow Canadian companies to strengthen their international competitiveness. This new marketplace will offer the framework for new business partnerships. It will strengthen North American business on the global stage.

Our participation in a successful North American Free Trade Agreement will guarantee that Canada continues to be a prime investment location for investors from around the world. It will demonstrate to investors that investing in this country will guarantee secure access to all three markets. It will serve as a signal to investors that Canada is positioning itself to secure its future prosperity. . . .

Mexico's trade barriers have hampered Canadian exporters' efforts to compete for a slice of the Mexican market of 85 million people. In announcing in February our intentions to join the talks, Canada wanted to ensure that Canadian exporters enjoy the same access to the Mexican market as do U.S. exporters. If we had not moved to join the talks, a bilateral U.S.-Mexico trade deal would have created preferential access for the U.S. and stacked the deck against Canadian business and our economy.

While Mexico has already reduced many tariffs as part of its decision to join the GATT in 1986, I remind you that its GATT-bound rate—the maximum levy it is allowed under the GATT—is 50 per cent for most products. The average rate of tariff protection is currently much lower than that. But Mexico holds in reserve the ability to resume a high-tariff policy. Today there is no treaty preventing the Mexican government from unilaterally raising its tariff above current rates, as it did in 1990 when the duty on numerous paper products went from 10 to 15 per cent. The ability to take such actions does not contribute to a stable trading environment. The phased elimination of duties through a new treaty will go a long way to creating confidence for Canadian exporters in the Mexican market.

Tariff barriers are not the only obstacle that concerns us in these negotiations; there are non-tariff barriers as well. In the early 1980s, almost all exports to Mexico required an import licence, one of the most common and effective forms of non-tariff barrier. Their discretionary nature makes them particularly damaging to a predictable trade environment. While that situation has changed for the better, with the requirement for licensing declining substantially, the barrier still affects approximately 20 per cent by value of Mexican imports. The licences apply to agricultural and some forest products, motor vehicles and selected chemicals and petrochemicals. These are all important export goods for Canada. The removal of these barriers would be a major element of a successful agreement.

These negotiations may also offer some modest opportunity to build on the gains made under the Canada-U.S. FTA and improve our access to the market of the United States. . . .

We strongly believe an agreement will encourage Canadians to form the strategic alliances in North America that can give our businesses the needed edge to meet and beat tough off-shore competition. . . .

Working closely with Mexican firms will also help Canadian business to strengthen contacts and alliances with the as yet untapped market of Latin America and South America. Latin America is on the move as never before. . . .

Our association with Mexican business may pay large dividends in years to come.

It is evident that Canadian firms can benefit from the lower-cost inputs of the Mexican marketplace.

The road to development is through trade, not aid. The result of a three-country economic partnership, in which each country relies on its own comparative advantage, will be increased trade and increased prosperity—and not only for companies, but for their workers as well.

SELECT BIBLIOGRAPHY

This short bibliography emphasizes material which has not already been referred to in either the notes or the readings of this book.

Chapter 1

A recent restatement of the classical theory of free trade can be found in Jagdish Bhagwati, *Protectionism* (Cambridge: MIT Press, 1988). The case for managed trade is made by Gunnar Myrdal, *The Challenge of World Poverty* (New York: Putman, 1970). The various theories of international integration are summarized in Charles Pentland, *International Theory and European Integration* (New York: Free Press, 1973). The best recent summary of the pro- and anti-free trade arguments as they apply to the United States in the late 20th century is Robert Lawrence and Charles Schultze, eds., *An American Trade Strategy: Options for the 1990s*. (Washington: Brookings Institution, 1990).

Chapter 2

Richard N. Cooper, "Trade Policy as Foreign Policy," in Robert W. Stern, ed., *U.S. Trade Policy in a Changing World Economy* (Cambridge: MIT Press, 1988, 291–321) gives a good summary of the history of US tariff policy. Canadian tariff history is covered in Kenneth Norrie and Douglas Owram, *A History of the Canadian Economy* (Toronto: Harcourt, Brace Javonovich, 1991). The best single history of the Canada-United States free trade issue is that by Jack Granatstein, "Free Trade: the History of an Issue," in Michael Henderson, ed., *The Future on the Table. Canada and the Free Trade Issue* (North York: Masterpress, 1987, 1–34). Much of the same history (and much more) can be found in Edelgard Mahant and Graeme Mount, *An Introduction to Canadian-American Relations* (Toronto: Nelson, 1989).

Chapter 3

The history of the negotiations of the FTA can be found in an excellent new book, G. Bruce Doern and Brian W. Tomlin, *Faith and Fear. The Free Trade Story*. (Toronto: Stoddard, 1991). The *New York Times* and *Washington Post* gave the story occasional coverage. The background and setting for the agreement is discussed in the book by Mahant and Mount, referred to under Chapter 2 above. Peter Morici, "U.S. Canadian-Trade Relations," in Peter Karl Kresl, ed. *Seen from the South* (Salt Lake City: Brigham Young University, 1989, 75–132) gives an American view of Canadian trade policy.

Chapter 4

There are many summaries of the FTA, but most of them, such as those prepared by firms of trade lawyers for their clients, are not readily accessible. The following four quite general summaries should not be too hard to locate: *Business America*, the entire January 30, 1989 issue; United States, Department of State, Bureau of Public Affairs, *U.S.-Canada Free Trade Agreement* Washington: July 1989 (a pamphlet which may be purchased for $1.00(US); "The Terms of the Deal," *Maclean's*, Nov. 21, 1988, supplement; *The Toronto Star*, Dec. 15, 1987, B1–B8. Marc Gold and David Leyton-Brown, eds., *Trade-Offs on Free Trade. The Canada-United States Free Trade Agreement* (Toronto: Carswell, 1988) consists of a number of articles which give a detailed summary and explanation of the FTA, topic by topic.

Chapter 5

There are only two accounts of how the FTA became law. The first is a chronology which appeared in *The Toronto Star* on December 31, 1988; the other can be found in the book by Doern and Tomlin, mentioned under Chapter 3 above. The main source for the American arguments for and against the FTA is the *Congressional Record*, for August 9, 1988 (House of Representatives) and September 19, 1988 (Senate). The hearings of the Subcommittee on Trade of the Committee on Ways and Means of the House of Representatives, for February 9, 26, and 29, and March 1, 11, and 25, 1988 give a more detailed picture of the opponents and proponents. In Canada, two of the many House of Commons debates on the FTA were held on June 21 and August 30, 1988; see, Canada, House of Commons, *Debates* (Ottawa: 1988), pp. 16647–16699 and 19045–19092. The major Canadian books for and against the FTA are mentioned in the notes to Chapter 5.

Chapters 6 and 7

Studies of the implementation and effects of the FTA are heavily colored by the writer's stand, for or against the Agreement. On the "for" side, the best single survey is that in the Royal Bank's *Econoscope* magazine for February 1991. For an American point of view, there is the April 8, 1991 issue of *Business America*, published by the U.S. Department of Commerce. Somewhat more neutral but leaning towards the "for" side is Strategico's "Year Two of the Canada-U.S. Free Trade Agreement," printed by the firm's Ottawa head office in December 1990. On the "against" side, there is the Centre for Policy Alternatives' report, Andrew Jackson, "Job Losses in Manufacturing," 1989–1991, (Ottawa: August 1991), photocopy. Also against but somewhat less partisan is the report by the Standing Committee on Foreign Affairs of the Senate of Canada, *Monitoring the Implementation of the Canada-United States Free Trade Agreement* (Ottawa: November 1990).

On the Canada-United States-Mexico NAFTA, a good analysis of the American reasons for entering into these negotiations can be found in Jeffrey Schott, *More Free Trade Areas?* (Washington: Institute for International Economics, 1989). A similar academic analysis of the Canadian position is Michael Hart, *A North American Free Trade Agreement. The Strategic Implications for Canada* (Ottawa: Centre for Trade Policy and Law, 1990). A Mexican academic explains his country's point of view in Gerardo M. Bueno, "A Mexican View," in William Diebold Jr., ed., *Bilateralism, Multilateralism and Canada in U.S. Trade Policy* (Cambridge, Ballinger, 1988, 109–128). Roderick Hill and Ronald Wonnacott, "Free Trade with Mexico: What Form Should It Take?" *C.D. Howe Commentary*, no. 28, March 1991, discuss how a trilateral agreement might mesh with the existing FTA.

INDEX